INTRODUCT

When we drove our newly purchase occurred to me that I had never, ever been next thought that went through my mind was, "Wow, we just spent a LOT of money. I sure hope I am going to like this…"

All our married life, my husband Joe and I had two goals for retirement: First of all, we wanted to live on the property my grandparents had purchased in 1948 at Pine Lake, Michigan. Secondly, we hoped to be in good enough health to travel extensively and do it by RV.

For many years, our only hobby was going to every RV Show, RV dealer promotional days and RV event we could find. We ate a lot of free hot dogs and we climbed in and out of many, many campers of every kind. *We* never bought anything but a number of friends who accompanied us did.

In time, we observed that most people end up buying three RVs. For example, if they started out with a motor home they'd probably stick with motor homes but it would take three purchases to finally end up with what they really wanted. We wanted to figure out what we wanted the first time: looking at units, talking to people and finally, by being really honest with each other,

We ruled out travel trailers early on. Joe didn't want to tow one. We were pretty sold on the 5th wheel until we test drove a truck big enough to haul one and my back hurt so much that I could barely crawl out of the passenger seat when we got back to the dealership. That left us with motor homes. The Class C is more like driving a van and overall, a less expensive way to go. Unfortunately, the ones we took on test drives were really rough riding. One in particular was like traveling inside a cement mixer. The Class A with its "bus" styling, comfortable ride and huge front window started to look like the clear choice.

We listened to all the helpful folks we met. Everyone had an opinion and they were more than happy to share their preferences. By the time we were ready to get serious we knew we didn't want much bigger than a 32' motor home. We weren't sure about the slide outs but we were open minded about that. We knew we wanted a sofa and a chair, a queen bed with room to walk around it and that we didn't care about a washer and dryer or upgrades like granite countertop.

With all the preparation, thought and planning, we pretty much found our dream home on wheels thanks to divine providence and dumb luck. I still feel absolutely blessed to have found the right thing for us the first time around. Not that we haven't had problems! If you consider that you are basically driving a house down the road, well – things are going to happen. Still, all things considered, we couldn't have found anything that would work any better for us.

And with the right equipment, a lot of trip planning and the enthusiasm of novices, we started out on what, so far, has been the adventure of a lifetime. But let me tell you how we came to buy the "Flamingo Express".

Chapter 1

February 2009   A Dream Comes True

We always thought that when we retired we would buy an RV, pack it up and make a 2000 mile trip our first time out. We had little interest in "camping" per se, no plans to camp near our home and certainly no time to take a vacation while my husband, Joe was self-employed with no one to man the office when he was away. So, we didn't see any point in buying the RV until we could actually use it.

That was until a cold winter's day in February 2009 when I happened to leaf through my husband's favorite reading material: the free car magazine he liked to pick up once a week at the gas station. Now, keep in mind that I hardly ever bothered to read it and when I did, I rarely saw any RV's. As I flipped through the pages, one ad caught my eye. A dealer in Indiana just over the border from us here in Michigan had a small photo ad with several nearly new Class A RVs at a price I couldn't believe. I thought there had to be something wrong but they were a major name brand and they looked GREAT in the ad. I told Joe I thought we should check it out. He was less than enthusiastic. His first reaction was the same as mine: too good to be true. He had a full day planned for Saturday, so I set the ad aside and pretty much decided we'd just forget it.

That Saturday dawned bright and clear. It was one of those amazing Michigan winter days with crystal blue skies, bright sun and crisp fresh air. About mid-morning I said to Joe, "We should really just drive down to Indiana and look at those RVs." To my surprise Joe told me he was already finished up with what he wanted to do and said, "Why not?"

The RV dealer specialized mostly in travel trailers. Remember, 2009 was in the midst of the economic downturn. Elkhart, Indiana, home of the RV industry, was practically closed for business. This dealer had ended up with the entire inventory of a Michigan dealer who had gone bankrupt and frankly, they had wanted the trailers; not so much the motor homes. Basically, they wanted to unload the motor homes as cheaply as they could as fast as they could. Lucky us!

We opened the door to the first motor home from the ad: 33' Class A with two slide outs and every single feature we had on our 'must have' list! The price was right but we also wanted to check out their several Class A's with no slides. Wow! Once we'd been in that 33' with the slides, the rest of them looked really cramped and unappealing. We took a second look at what was now the only Class A with slides that was left – the one we'd seen first and really loved. We still couldn't believe the price and kept thinking there must be a catch!

Let me just tell you something here: my husband and I just DO NOT make a decision without sleeping on it and praying about it. We have pretty much always figured that if something was right for us, it would be there when we decided. We walked into the dealer showroom and sat down with the salesman to talk price. Nope, they wouldn't come down a cent (not surprising when the unit was $18,000 below the listed WHOLESALE)…I looked at Joe. He looked at me. We both said the same thing: If we don't buy this, we're never buying an RV….We signed on the bottom line right then and there.

Another salesperson stopped by to see if we were buying. Seems he had someone on the phone that had looked at that very same unit in the morning and now decided he wanted to buy it. Well, unfortunate for that other person but YAY! for us. That night we slept like little lambs without a moment of buyer's remorse.

A few days later we drove back to Indiana and became the proud owners of a Class A motor home in the dead of winter with no plans to camp in it any time soon but we couldn't have been happier –

except for that small detail that neither one of us knew the first thing about camping!

Chapter 2

Summer 2009 - The Adventures Begin

Every time we looked out the kitchen window and spotted the big bus in our backyard we grinned like lunatics … there it was, just waiting for us to retire and hit the road. I busily made lists of everything I could possibly think of that we might need in our travels. Our laundry room began to fill up with totes, boxes and piles of things I thought we'd pack for our home on wheels. We came up with a name-The Flamingo Express-based on my Flamingo collection and the idea that our first trip would be to Florida (it wasn't).

My dear friend since grade school, Kathy, and her husband Jim invited us to go camping for a long weekend with them at a nearby campground where they kept their travel trailer for the summers. It sounded like a good way to have a 'shake-down cruise' and a good time. OH BOY! Take my word for it; you do NOT want to start your first RV adventure by loading up the rig and starting a 2000 mile trip, which was our original plan. Let me tell you, it was not a **good** plan. Again, we were SO lucky that it just worked out for us to do this short trip first! It was pretty much an adventure in finding out what all we didn't know!

Our first challenge was backing the motor home into a fairly small spot. We immediately learned the value of the "Pull Through" lot. Joe handled it off like a pro, only taking out one small clump of plants and otherwise pretty much getting it lined up on the first try.

Then Joe and Jim spent a good part of the weekend trying to figure out why we didn't have any hot water. Kathy must have suggested like, eight times, that they look for a bypass valve under the bathroom sink. Finally the guys had a bright idea! They should look under the bathroom sink! Sure enough, there was an access panel and behind the panel was a bypass valve for the hot water. Duh.

We had our first campfire, drank a lot of wine, had a lot of laughs and found out that we had a lot to learn about camping.

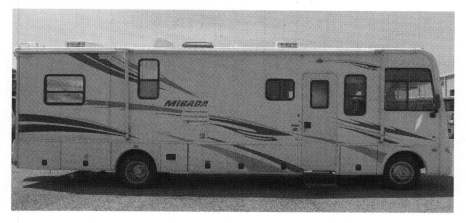

Our 1ˢᵗ and only Class A Motorhome

The First Longer Trip on our Own

After not having more than a day or two at a time off in the last six years we decided that we could manage a long weekend to try out the motor home with an "out of state" trip. We planned a Thursday through Monday out of the office and worked like insane squirrels trying to stash every last nut before getting out of the office for three work days. We loaded up the Flamingo Express on Wednesday night in anticipation of leaving early Thursday morning. Anticipation is the key word here. We were both so excited that we woke up well before 6 a.m. and couldn't get back to sleep. About seven we decided we may as well get going. That final packing up and getting out took a little longer than we had thought. At 10:45 a.m. we finally pulled onto our private street and lumbered over the potholes towards the open road. Joe maneuvered around our neighbor's overhanging roof that just about covers the road, squeezed by another neighbor's thoughtlessly placed fence and we were off.

We hadn't gone twenty miles before my entire left side was numb. Riding over Michigan roads for any length of time was like being in a milkshake mixer. I pulled a pillow off the sofa and propped it behind my aching back. Ahhh, that was better! We made frequent stops and Joe pulled the Express into the various parking spots like he had been doing it all his life. Hello Indiana! Hello Illinois! We were way ahead of schedule and decided to stop at an Air Museum in the little town of Rantoul, IL. There was plenty of room in the parking lot and we had over two hours before closing time so we figured we'd see what was there. Joe especially enjoyed the Vietnam era planes and helicopters. After about the first hour I'd seen the displays and had enough walking around looking at planes so I wandered back to the gift shop. The ladies there were really nice and very helpful. I think I got the senior discount even though I was not strictly speaking a "senior" yet.

It was almost closing time so we headed out to the motor home and consulted our directions to the campsite we had reserved for the night. I carefully put the location in the GPS, checked my written directions and we started out. After several turns we appeared to be on the right road but not in the right place. I saw a big flag up ahead and thought that must be it. Unfortunately that brought us to a dead end and the flag apparently belonged to a really big fan of the "Fighting Illini". Joe did a great job of turning around the Flamingo Express in tight quarters but we were definitely lost. I pulled out the cell phone and luckily got right through to the campground manager. Turned out the campground was right next to the Air Museum where we had been! We could have thrown a rock and hit it (well, almost).

We parked, hooked up and set about enjoying a beautiful evening marred only by the fact that about two or three million locust, cicadas or some related very, very noisy insects had infested all the nearby fields. It was still a nice night for a walk. We made a thorough exploration of the campground, Prairie Pines and enjoyed a beautiful sunset. We retired back to our own cozy little place to watch some TV. Joe remembered we'd need a converter box and proceeded to hook it up. All went well until he pulled the box out to more comfortably work on it-that's when the connecting cable snapped clean off and retracted down into the wall. Several cuss words and some minutes later Joe did manage to retrieve the cable, figure out a work around and we settled down to a little evening entertainment. It wasn't long before we were both yawning-the microwave mac and cheese gave us a sleepy carb load. That plus the excitement of our first day on the road and we were done for the night.

The next morning we both enjoyed a little light snack of coffee and doughnuts; not really very hungry. Anxious to be on the road again we packed up, fired up and started on the second leg of our journey to southern Illinois to see our longtime friends, Tim and Deb. Again Joe pulled out like a pro even though our "pull through" spot required going over a curb that was at least eight inches tall. Let's just say it was supposed to be "pull through".

We wound our way back to the highway and charted our next stop, a little scenic Amish community along the way. I spotted the sign and we pulled off the highway. Eight miles later I thought perhaps I'd seen the wrong sign. Friends of ours who have made the trip down US 57 many times recommended this little town as a great place to enjoy Amish made goods and also hit a nice Outlet Mall. We rolled into a tiny town that appeared to have been last modernized in 1912. Some good-hearted folks were standing right in the middle of the road (!) selling candy for a charitable cause. Joe asked them if we were in the right town and being assured that we were, we got directions to the Tourist Center. It was closed. With that we decided to just head back to the highway. One exit later we saw huge signs – Amish Buffet, Amish Furniture, Amish Shops, and Outlet Mall – this exit. Oh well, never mind.

We continued on to the next small town and enjoyed a home cooked lunch complete with hot, fresh bread and homemade apple butter. We discovered that we might be staying longer than we expected because the town's High School was holding the Homecoming Parade and the parade route was going right by the parking lot where we had left our motorhome. So, what else was there to do but watch the parade? There were three fire trucks, three floats, several cars carrying Homecoming Royalty and the smallest marching band I have ever seen. They wore matching red T-shirts and were comprised of one tuba, one baritone, a couple of drums and a girl playing the flute who appeared to be playing a totally and completely different tune than the rest of the band. The car rolled by carrying the "Miss --- Queen" and from her girth we deduced that she must have been elected by the pound...But she waved merrily and I'm sure she's a very sweet person. That was pretty much it, give or take a tractor and a hay wagon. It wasn't long before we were back on the road again. A few stops in between, a long slowdown for road repair and finally we pulled into our friends' driveway with our home on our backs like a couple of old turtles. It was great to see our friends and we enjoyed a couple of fabulous dinners out, the Air

Show at the Scott Air Force base, some good conversation and before we knew it-time to leave again!

Off to a bit of a late start Sunday afternoon. By the time I had gotten us totally and completely lost we had a good 45 minute delay. It's really hard to know where to go when you don't know where you are! Joe had the smart idea to put "home" in the GPS since we couldn't get it to find the campground where we were headed – and that worked! That got us back on the highway, only to once again hit construction. A light fog turned to drizzle, the drizzle to light rain and then to a downpour. Joe did a great job of driving in the dark but I think we've learned that we'll try to always make our campground in daylight whenever possible. We had good directions to the campground but it was pitch dark, I mean no streetlight, no mercury vapor lamp, and no light bulb hanging from a hollow tree–dark. We made two circuits of the campground before finding our spot and decided it was raining so hard that we would leave the living room slide in. After a snack and a few minutes of conversation we were both totally done for the night and happy to have our comfortable bed.

The next morning we met a fellow camper who told us that she and her husband had been "Full Timers" for three or four years. They lived in the same house for 43 years right there in the area and now camped summers in the local campground and spent the winter in Texas. She said they did keep a small storage unit and saved a few things like out of season clothes but almost everything had been sold. "Except the Christmas decorations," she said. "My husband kept those although I have no idea why." I know I couldn't give up my home base; my stuff needs a place to live.

After taking a walk through the entire campground we decided it was time to go. One thing we learned from other campers was to be sure to check that the exterior steps were retracted before hitting the road. Every time we pulled out with the motorhome I would ask Joe, "Are the steps up?" One of the common (and expensive) newbie mistakes is to take off with the steps out. We prepared to pull onto the main road when a couple began yelling, "Stop, stop!" I slid open my window to hear why they were trying to get our attention and fortunately, they had spotted our steps down! We stopped, pulled up the steps and started over again.

The trip home was uneventful. We discovered a major pastime is keeping the lookout for good prices on gasoline. Another is deciding whether to stop or hope for another rest area not too far down the road. Soon the "Welcome to Michigan" sign greeted us. We both thought we had done very well. It was a good "starter trip". Not too many days, pretty much flat with unchallenging driving conditions; we learned lot and avoided any real disasters. Then we got to our own backyard. We've been parking the Flamingo Express right next to our pole barn and Joe has gotten really good at swinging it in although there is limited space. He's done it countless times already without a hitch. Only this time somehow he smacked into the roof of the barn, bent the roof edge and whacked the corner of the motor home. I guess we'll be keeping it for sure now…it's no longer in perfect condition. But, hey- any landing you walk away from, right?

Chapter 3

Our First BIG Trip

Joe retired in October of 2011 and by then we had several "short" trips under our belts. We felt pretty secure that we had everything we needed in our home on wheels…and we had learned a lot. We'd purchased a tow bar set up for our trusty Jeep and learned that if you back up your RV with the car attached the tow bar will crumple like a cheap linen suit. (Not good). We discovered that the TV we didn't think was *that* important, uh, was. For some reason, it never occurred to us that it would get dark in the evenings and once you're in for the night there's not a whole lot of entertainment outside of TV and our small stock of videos. We also learned to download our day's pictures to the computer every night. If not, it didn't take long to forget exactly where we'd been and what we'd taken pictures of…

I'd spent a lot of time planning our first really big adventure, Michigan to Texas. I always look at it this way: if you're going someplace and you may never be there again (most likely), do you really want to get back home and have someone ask you, "Oh, wow! Did you see the World's Biggest Hot Dog when you were in _____?" And you'd have to admit that, no you missed that. I wanted to be sure we saw everything worth seeing and ate every regional dish, visited every landmark and generally didn't miss anything.

How could you miss seeing a giant squirrel??

Joe Retires and We Head Out for Texas

I spent most of the summer planning and in October of 2011 my husband retired from his full-time business. After a combination Retirement/65th birthday celebration for Joe with family and friends, we readied for our first big trip. On the first leg of our winding journey to the great state of Texas, we bummed a couple of nights for free in the driveway of friends in southern Illinois.

After some fun and great pizza with our friends we drove off through light rain and into the sun as we crossed into Arkansas and then Missouri. It was cotton picking time. Huge machines were sweeping over the flat fields of cotton as far as you could see. I had not known that cotton is baled up in what looks like the hay bales we see in fields in Michigan. The bales are covered in plastic and then taken by semi. Interesting.

We reached our destination for the night just as the sun set at 5 p.m.! We were a little disoriented with the change to CST and then another lost hour with the change from Daylight Savings Time to Standard Time, plus being on the very far eastern edge of the Central time zone it got dark really, really early.

The folks at Tom Sawyers RV Park were waiting for us and we followed "Jim" on his ATV down and around to the very edge of the mighty Mississippi River with a view of the Memphis bridge lit up and sparkling in the distance. Wow! We woke up in the morning to see a tug pushing a barge on the river-like an IMAX movie right out our front window. Very cool.

One recommendation: If you are on I-55, watch for signs for Lambert's Café. It's exit 76 if you are on 55 south. What a blast! And what a ton of food! We had two full meals, each–no kidding. The café is the home of "throwed rolls" and that's not referring to the preparation-that's the serving technique. A young man winds his way through the cafe (by the way, the place itself is a hoot; décor is license plates from all over) all of a sudden you'll hear a yell, "Hot rolls!" and the next thing you see someone puts a hand up in the air and a roll goes flying at him! Joe caught two for us and they were delicious: huge, tender yeast rolls, obviously homemade, and served with sorghum or apple butter. Every meal comes with "sides"-a huge list of southern specialties to choose from plus the servers come to your table with "pass arounds", a yummy macaroni and cheese with tomatoes dish, peppery fried potatoes and onions, fried okra and more. I had the ribs and they were great. A big roll of paper towels is on every rustic wooden table and is pretty much a necessity! Dinner was messy but delicious.

The next morning, we went for a walk on the extensive nature trail around the RV Park to try to burn off some of that terrific food we'd had and then it was on to the Memphis Zoo to see the Pandas!

On to the Natchez Trace

We spent a wonderful day at the zoo in Memphis although it was obvious we were "out of towners". Joe walked up to the entrance wearing shorts and a t-shirt and the ticket taker, who was wearing a winter coat, looked at us like we were nuts. Hey, it was WARM by Michigan standards! The zoo was delightful and the pandas were winsome and comical. We enjoy zoos, so it was worth the time. The bridge to Memphis is really beautiful and we enjoyed seeing it lit up again on our last night there before heading to Clinton, Mississippi the following day.

We entered the Natchez Trace Parkway just off I-20 after spending the night in a "campground" – and I use the term loosely. Springridge RV Park in Clinton was basically a parking lot in the middle of a trailer park. We were so close to the next campers I wasn't sure we'd have room to put out our slides so we could get into bed! But it was ok for an overnight stop.

The Natchez Parkway is a linear National Park, closed to commercial traffic with a speed limit of 50 miles an hour. There are no services on the parkway, so gas up before you get on. You'll have to get off the Trace for restaurants; however there are picnic areas along the way.

All our experiences are filtered through our own personalities, likes and dislikes. We found the Trace to be a delightful, relaxing drive through acres of wooded scenery with many points of interest to explore. Especially in the fall, traffic is practically non-existent and on this particular day the sun filtered softly through the changing colors with an occasional shower of leaves coming down as though nature had tossed gold coins on us from above. Two deer came out in the dappled sunlight to pose, still as lawn statues as we passed by. A wild turkey made an appearance. It was a day to remember.

Or, if you are my friend Charlene, the Natchez Trace is a boring two lane road with trees the same as she can see in her backyard. There isn't a Casino or 4 star restaurant anywhere in sight. Booooring. So, it just depends on what you enjoy.

We got out at the site of the Sunken Trace, the original pathway used by animals to get to the salt licks up by Nashville, Tennessee and later followed by man. I could almost hear the soft tread of animals and the swish of moccasin feet in the dry leaves, from days gone by. The sense of history is heightened by numerous sites of battles and other historic points of interest. We think it is one of America's most unusual National Parks and well worth a leisurely visit. I wish we had known there is a really nice campground there, too. But we continued on to Natchez where we were staying in Vidalia at Riverview RV Park for three nights.

Natchez, Mississippi

We've been to Natchez before and really enjoy the area. It is particularly rich in traditional homes of the south as it was one city not laid waste by the Union army. Before the War Between the States, there were more millionaires in Natchez than any other city in the country. Cotton was king and the "king" made many a rich man; those men built splendid homes that still stand today. After the Civil War, the resulting poverty acted as a preservation tool – people couldn't afford new things. Many amazing period pieces still reside in these old homes and there are incredible finds in local antique shops. The Catholic Church is also worth seeing. Originally the Cathedral of Mississippi, it contains priceless works of art and the building itself rivals the churches of Europe.

In the meantime, I managed to develop a sinus infection. After five days of suffering I finally fessed up to Joe that I needed to find a Prompt Care Clinic. You know, one of those places where "Prompt" means you wait for hours… Joe enjoyed reading the magazines while I saw a doctor who looked about old enough to have graduated medical school last week. He was probably much older than I thought and likely married to one of the southern belles we had seen around Natchez. There appears to be an entire class of women who lunch, shop and wear diamond engagement rings so big that you wonder how they hold up their hands. We toured one antebellum home which is now a Bed and Breakfast and got a fast shuffle through because there was a big luncheon meeting there the same day. The women who showed up would have been overdressed for a Gala Ball in Michigan. I can't remember the last time I saw a brocade dress, much less in the middle of the day. And the gossip flew fast and furious. Yikes.

One thing we did enjoy immensely was the Monmouth Mansion tour. The ladies there couldn't believe we were eligible for the senior discount. The one must have asked Joe three times, "And you're sixty-five?" she shook her head and muttered, "My, my, my." Kind of flattering.

Monmouth was very interesting as are all of the home and plantation tours – a real look into the past. Many operate as hotels or B and B's. The upkeep alone must be a killer.

A few miles out of Natchez we toured a working cotton plantation, Frogmore. It offered a nice exhibit with a video presentation of the original planters and how they lived and then a tour of actual buildings from the period. As I often reflect, life back then was often short and brutal. It is not unusual to see entire families buried together all having died of yellow fever within a few days of each other or six or eight children of a family all having been lost before the age of one or two. Common childhood diseases ended children's short lives. Touring old cemeteries gives new meaning to "only the strong survive"…it's a wonder anyone lived long enough to accomplish anything in life! The tour included a look at present day cotton operations. All the harvesting of cotton in the U.S is now mechanized. Talk about back breaking labor to have picked that stuff by hand and separate out the seeds! The darn seeds stick to the "lint" like ticks on a bloodhound! Today, China is the world's leading cotton producer.

We left the Natchez area for Cajun country and soon saw signs advertising the "BEST" boudin and "BEST" cracklins – apparently anyone can claim to be the "BEST". Naturally we had to try some of the local cuisine and we stopped at-you guessed it – BEST Market between Duson and Lafayette.

They were doing a brisk business in the meat market: quail, alligator, pork (cuts I've never heard of), and of course, boudin. Boudin is a mixture of spices, sausage and rice stuffed into a casing, well, like sausage. We tried the boudin balls which were crispy fried balls of boudin rolled in a mixture of spices and dried bread crumbs. Hot, hot, hot!! You definitely want your cold drink at the ready. The cracklins are basically pork rinds. We passed on those and also the quail eggs.

Fortified by Cajun Home Cooking, we went to meet Bryan of Champagne's Cajun Swamp Tours. Bryan is one crazy Cajun guy, let me tell you. The tour is advertised as "handicapped accessible" but getting to the boat was barely able-bodied accessible! And getting to the boat was only the beginning of the hair-raising adventure. What this guy does to a Mercury outboard motor would make any boater cringe. It drove Joe crazy. This guy went over trees, logs, into three inches of water, blew mud up fourteen feet high and forged on through swamp as if he were in a swan boat in Central Park New York City. Yikes. He also thought it was amusing to speed up to a sleepy alligator and to see if the gator would jump. It made me nervous when Bryan whacked a gator with a tree limb but the big guy just kept on eyeing us with his cold reptilian stare so I decided we were probably more or less safe. The tour of Lake Martin and the surrounding swamp was about two hours but at various times when we were stuck in mud I thought it might be two days. Luckily, even in the middle of nowhere, Bryan received and made several cell phone calls (while driving the boat) so I guess someone could have come to find us. I can't imagine what the German couple with us thought. They only spoke a little bit of English but they didn't appear to be very concerned. Maybe they thought that was what all Americans do - run around the swamp whacking alligators.

Beautiful (?) Lake Martin

Louisiana

We stayed two nights at Frog City RV Park in Duson, Louisiana and it was one of those places where their website was better than the actual park. But it was okay and we had no real complaints. Next we made our way to our final destination for this leg of the trip: Lake Charles. The RV park was just newly opened and the owner and manager went out of their way to make us welcome.

Christmas decorations were up in town and the beautiful homes near the lake had obviously all been professionally decorated. That alone was worth the time spent exploring the area. We also got a big kick out of the Mardi Gras museum and I even snuck on one of the outlandish headdresses when the curator wasn't looking-what a hoot.

Our last day in Lake Charles was devoted to cleaning and prepping the motor home to store it on site when we drove back to Michigan for Thanksgiving and Christmas. As it turned out, we unexpectedly had an early start to the day when the huge diesel pusher next to us revved up the engine early in the morning, waking us up. Joe looked out to see if the guy was just warming up or what. The next thing we see is the motor home pulling out with the electrical cord still attached and the electric box being pulled right out of the ground! You know, sometimes I feel kind of stupid that I still go over my checklist every time we leave but right then I didn't feel so dumb. One of the maintenance people saw the guy take off and chased him down.

As you leave the 12 Oaks RV Park in St. Charles the sign says:

- o STEPS UP?
- o ANTENNAE DOWN?
- o WIFE ON BOARD?

I guess they should have added: Electric line unplugged?

Well, we unplugged, packed up the Jeep, made final arrangements for storage of the RV and headed back to Michigan by way of Natchitoches, Louisiana to enjoy the Festival of Lights there – a great way to start the holidays as we made our way back home.

Before we left, however, Joe had a moment of misgiving about where the motor home was going to be parked. It appeared to us that it was pretty soft soil at the back of the park where we were storing. I'm not sure the folks there had actually done any storage before but they assured us it was "high and dry" and it would be fine. Uh oh.

Chapter 4

Stuck!

We made it back to Louisiana to get the motor home; good news! The bad news: it was stuck in the mud. After a 3 year drought there had been a huge rainfall in the past week. The high and dry area where we left the Flamingo Express was a mucky mire. Joe spent at least two hours on the phone getting the tow set up but good news (again)-at least we were out with no damage to the coach. And then the bad news-RV Park was full. Since the owners had assured us that we didn't need a reservation for our return, they had us camp in the owner's driveway and they even ran an electrical cord for us so we had partial power. In the morning we headed off towards Galveston, Texas.

Before I forget, we had stopped at a Wendy's for an afternoon break on the second day driving to Lake Charles. It was on a busy highway with a huge Walmart superstore behind it. Right off the parking lot was a small drainage ditch with some water and vegetation but certainly not what you could call a "pond"... I spotted something brown and furry looking. Thinking it was a dead animal in there I almost looked away but then I noticed how healthy and shiny the fur looked-and there were 4 pairs of eyes looking up at me. Yikes. Turns out they were nutria-whoa...like hamsters on steroids. Hard to believe that these things could live between the Walmart and Wendy's parking lot right off a four lane highway. Who knew?

Anyway, on the road to Galveston the GPS sent us by way of Egypt...or somewhere. A 2 hour trip took about 4 ½ hours. We got totally lost (that part was on us,-ok, **me**-not the GPS). Good news (again)-found the RV Park before dark and got into our spot. That's when we realized we had ruined a tire. I mean, do I *really* have to insert the words "bad news"?? So our next adventure will be finding someplace to buy a tire and get it put on the bus. We just found out that the Houston Olympic qualifying race and the Houston Marathon are tomorrow. So even if we're not stuck here waiting for the tire, we will not be going to Houston this weekend. Luckily there are plenty of other destinations nearby. Unfortunately, it turns out that our park is not exactly on the beach as we had thought. Also, the weather is pretty chilly here (30's for the a.m. tomorrow) but it's really quite nice and hey! We are not shoveling snow!

Tire Repaired and the Fun Begins

It has been a great few days with none of that cold, white stuff I had mentioned. The weather has been a little bit unseasonably warm with temps running about 10 degrees higher than average for the Galveston/Houston/Austin areas. Apparently from the lack of crowds at all the venues we've been to and the availability of RV Park space, most people go much farther south for winter in Texas. For us, this has been great. We toured Moody Park in Galveston on Tuesday and practically had the place to ourselves. The complex there is three giant pyramids: one housing a first class aquarium, one with a botanical garden and a third that we didn't tour, which features an IMAX theatre and more natural history type exhibits. Moody Aquarium was really outstanding with several displays that took the visitor below and above the water. The "tunnel" area allows you to be surrounded by mantas, sharks, sea turtles and amazing fish. The Gardens were very lovely and featured a Butterfly House that has three floors of various types of gardens with pools, water features and exotic birds. So relaxing-and no long lines or crowds! Plus we had a fabulous lunch in the Garden Restaurant overlooking the Bay. I had a shrimp salad that was a bed of greens, two avocado halves smothered with whole shrimp blended with a perfectly seasoned, herbed dressing and garnished with vegetable slices – enough for two people, really. Follow that up with a glorious slice of chocolate mousse cake covered in a decadent fudge frosting…wow. Worth every calorie.

We have found Galveston to be very interesting, and really much less 'ugly' than we thought. It is definitely more industrial with the petrochemical industry and refineries are all over the place. The one thing I found worrisome is the water in this area. You probably know I am a big proponent of not using bottled water and at most, filtering your own water if needed. Not here! Oh, brother…I can't even get the water up to my mouth for the smell. Yuck. I've never tasted anything like it. Even after filtering it is nauseating. It has a smell of rotting swamp and tastes about like it smells. We are amazed that with all the birds and waterfowl you see everywhere here drinking the water and swimming around in brackish, nasty looking ponds that everything doesn't hatch out with two heads or something. I would definitely recommend buying bottled drinking water to use for cooking, tooth brushing and drinking. Anything that smells and tastes this bad can't possibly be good for you.

Today we got an introduction to Houston traffic. Wow. Rush hour is brutal. Can't imagine living like that and making a commute of one or two hours every day. The Houston Zoo is pretty much right downtown, adjacent to the Hermann Park, Houston's largest green space. When we entered the Zoo today an employee invited us to get out of the cold for a few minutes under the warming lights they had there… and it was like 72 degrees! We thought he was nuts. Joe was wearing a short sleeve t-shirt and we thought it was totally pleasant. Matter of fact, by the end of the day we were a little too warm.   It is not the largest zoo we've seen but nicely done with an emphasis on education, conservation and raising awareness of endangered and threatened species. One interesting exhibit was in the Primate area. We were talking to one of the docents, who told us the Orangutan we were seeing was a "hybrid".

Seems there were two species of Orangutan in adjoining enclosures. The zoo personnel were not aware that the two would interbreed in the first place, much less when the two animals were separated by iron bars. Just goes to show where there's a will there's a way…Hmm.   I'm guessing they installed tighter fencing between exhibits after that. Overall it was a nice zoo. Two of the elephants have babies and that was especially endearing to see.

Yesterday we spent the day at the Space Center. When planning to go there I found it somewhat confusing…was it a theme park or a government installation? Turns out it is sort of both. The Center is a great "hands on" venue that can be an entire day trip to see. The tram that runs from the Center is NOT a theme park ride, it is a "no nonsense, go through a check point, have your bags examined" deal that takes you on a tour of the actual working NASA complex. It was very well done and extremely interesting. Again, the lines were non-existent and there was no waiting for any of the many featured attractions there. This is definitely the off season here, but it is right on for us!

There are many more attractions in the Galveston/Houston area, just be aware that there may be shorter hours or reduced days of operation in January and February. Tomorrow I think we're going to take a lazy day and maybe just drive over to the beach with a picnic. Temps should be in the mid-seventies tomorrow, perfect picnic weather as far as Michiganders are concerned. Since our tire fiasco which deflated our tire and our bank account, everything else has been working fine on the Flamingo Express. We are not finding that we want to move around as much as we had expected.

The park we are in now, Bay RV in San Leon, is well located to both Galveston and Houston. It is very nice, quiet and well-priced. So we decided to stay a second week here and continue to tour nearby. We were definitely unrealistic about how much time to spend in an area.

We have a week in the Austin area planned next, then on to San Antonio for about 10 days, then Corpus Christi. It seems unlikely we will go all the way down to where most snowbirds go, the semi-tropical area near the border of Mexico: Brownsville and McAllen. Really, Texas could be four separate trips: the Gulf Coast, Northern Texas/Dallas Fort Worth, West Texas and Big Bend National Park and Southern Texas.

Chapter 5

Happy in Houston

If bling is your thing, you must get to the permanent collection of the Houston Natural History Museum and see the Gem collection. Can you say fabulous? The displays of natural stones are gorgeous enough but the collection of jewelry is absolutely eye popping. Need I say there was a tiara there that was just my style….wow! Unfortunately, the jewels are in a big, thick, solid, freaking vault; no checking stuff out for overnight. Bummer.

We enjoyed the entire Museum and on Tuesday after 2 p.m. entry is free. There is a charge for the planetarium and for special exhibits, but the permanent collection easily took up four full hours without doing anything extra.

Houston has many fine dining opportunities, but frankly, we were just too put off by the traffic to try to find a restaurant in the city. The rush hour starts at 3-4 p.m. and goes until 8 p.m. Frequently the whole thing was one big sea of tail lights, or else a parking lot. I don't know how people live like that.

We opted to go back to the little community of San Leon to "Bubba's". It had been recommended as a great place for shrimp. Their specialty is 'endless shrimp'. We didn't think we had better stuff down endless amounts of shrimp, but we did go with the shrimp dinner. Hard to believe that fresh shrimp caught the same day makes so much better eating than what we usually get up north, even in a good restaurant. Bubba's has great ambiance and overlooks the bay, which is all cool, but the food – Wow.

Monday we took a drive down to the Brazonia area which is to the south. We visited a Natural Wildlife refuge and fish hatchery which was actually closed on Mondays, but the habitat trails were available and pretty much deserted. There is a lovely boardwalk that keeps you up and away from the snakes and alligators (yes, we did see an alligator sunning himself again-eek). We also took advantage of the deserted public beach at Surfside. The hard packed white sand made a great place to walk along the Gulf. We returned by way of Galveston, taking the toll bridge that brings you to the south end of the island. It was an enjoyable day and good timing as two days later a storm ripped through the area taking down trees, tearing off roofs and bringing driving rain and hail. Yup, timing is everything!

From San Leon on to Rockport, Texas

We left San Leon and the Houston/Galveston area about 11:30 in the morning. We find that driving through mid-day with a late afternoon destination works pretty well for us. A) I am not an early riser and it takes at least 3 cups of coffee before I begin to recognize my surroundings, B) It takes a while yet for us to do all the little "getting ready to leave" chores, stowing items, dumping, double checking our check list, triple checking our check list…you get the picture   C) We have long since discovered why you rarely see big rigs on the road after dark. It is not fun getting into a space and hooked up in total blackness, which is what you find in some parks after sundown.

Joe's parents wintered in Texas for many years which was rather stunning as it seemed totally out of character for both of them. At home in Michigan they were loners with no friends, a couple of close neighbors and a very, very occasional visit with relatives. Hard to believe they had a fabulous time every winter in an RV park with their trailer. Now I can see why Ma and Pa got down to the Rio Grande valley as quickly as possible. The most remarkable thing about Texas landscape here is that it is totally unremarkable. Once the novelty of seeing a palm tree or a cactus wears off, this is one boring landscape. The monotony of our trip here was broken up however, when our GPS lady stopped talking to Joe again. That happens every so often, and I think it's because Joe really ticks her off by ignoring her on a regular basis. Anyway, the audio mysteriously quit and Joe missed a turn. Thinking we would just take the next indicated turn, no problem, we got on what I would loosely term a 'road' that was barely one lane, and that one lane was fast disappearing in the encroaching vegetation coming from both sides. The next turn would take us on a two track that appeared to end not far in the distance. We chose to stay on the one lane. Good choice. We didn't see a blessed thing on the entire road except circling buzzards, so we were relieved when we somehow stumbled back onto to Highway 35.

Speaking of buzzards, we have been following the Texas Migration Birding trail off and on all the way down the coast. So far we've seen hawks on every telephone pole, and turkey buzzards. That's about it. Today we are going to a famous nature area, the Aransas National Wildlife Park. Supposedly the nearly extinct whooping cranes gather here for the winter. Well, we'll just see about that...

Birding Continues

Rather than drive 'til we dropped to go from San Leon to Mission Texas, we broke up the trip with a luxurious 3 day, 2 night stay at beautiful Rockport, Texas. Ok, maybe not luxurious....but the park is supposed to be the "best" in the area. It was definitely one of the more expensive! We are getting a feel for how people choose to stay in a particular park. There are parks that suit us just fine: clean, safe, quiet and laundry available. That's because we are traveling and just using the park for a home base. The "Winter Texans" are mostly looking for activities, community and social opportunities. The park in Rockport offered a full slate of activities all day and evening, every day of the week. We met a couple who had wintered there for six years, mainly because they enjoy dancing and this park has live music and dancing every weekend. There were shuffleboard tournaments, poker games, organized exercise classes, open swim, a community church service on Sunday – something for everyone. However, the RVs are packed in so close together I felt claustrophobic. It wouldn't be my choice for staying a number of months.

Speaking of phobias, if you suffered from Kenophobia you really wouldn't want to live in Texas. Talk about "wide open spaces". I thought Indiana and Illinois were flat in places! Here you can see until the horizon drops off. You don't have to stare in the distance for too long before you start seeing mirages. I cannot for the life of me figure out how or why anyone originally came to this God forsaken part of the country. There's a famous quote we've seen a number of times down here, attributed to Davy Crockett, "You can all go to Hell; I'm going to Texas". My question is: how could he tell the difference?

There is dust, scrub, cows, more dust, cactus, more dust, a few major roads and two tracks. So, we were excited to get to Mission, Texas in the semi-tropical part of the state. We pictured idyllic palm trees swaying in the breeze, bright blooming flowers, lush groves of orange, grapefruit and lemons. Yikes. The area from Brownsville to McAllen and Mission is like one big humongous non-stop strip mall. We couldn't tell when we left one area and drove into the next. Our RV Park does feature a birding area, some bushes in bloom and palm trees. It also has poisonous black widow spiders, a gate that is locked from 8 p.m. to 8 a.m. and gang graffiti on everything that doesn't move. We've been advised that much of the area here near the border of Mexico is not very safe. I guess we'll find out. We are just a few blocks from a major migratory bird center. That should be nice. We are looking forward to going to the various parks and over to South Padre Island.

While at Rockport, we took a day to go to Aransas National Wildlife Refuge. We first spotted two alligators right off the bat, then that was about the end of our exotic sightings. We walked on several birding trails only to see Northern Cardinals (have those), blackbirds (have those), and the ubiquitous hawks, which are on every dead tree and telephone pole here. We were joking about how the birding had been better in our back yard at Pine Lake than in a world famous migratory preserve. Then we walked out to a trail with a good overview of the fresh water and the intercostal waterway beyond. I trained our field glasses on some white blobs way out on a sand bar. Unbelievably, it was the several of the nearly extinct Whooping Cranes! Actually, it was eight of them! There are only 479 known in existence in 2011. Ok, if we don't see another bird, I'm alright with that.

Chapter 6

Mission, Texas

The Americana RV Park here is known for birding. I found out yesterday that the green parrots that frequent the park are best spotted early in the morning. I guess I won't be seeing a green parrot. But, I am looking forward to visiting the State Park a few blocks from here that is a favorite spot for seeing migratory birds and butterflies. That is, when we actually get a chance to do something here in the area.

In the meantime, I've been doing laundry, shopping to restock the pantry and a few other domestic chores. That is partly due to the intermittent sprinkles here and partly due to Joe's Big Project. Oh, boy. We noticed some water leaking around our shower enclosure the last two times we started on the road after being camped for more than a couple of days.

Now, I should explain that I am not good at the "camping" experience. I hated taking showers in Gym class 45 years ago and I'm not any more cheerful now about taking a shower where other flip-flops have tread before me. Also, I am not very good at balancing on one leg like my flamingo friends, while I try to dry one foot. If I put a bare foot on the public shower floor, I can just feel the athlete's foot fungus crawling towards it, eek. Also, my organizational skills (or lack of) just about guarantee that I will end up at the bathhouse missing either underwear, shampoo, soap or some other essential. This time it was soap. Hopefully, washing one's entire body with Head and Shoulders shampoo is not harmful. Anyway...we usually shower in our coach, so the water puddling was pretty worrisome. Having the floor rot would be a big problem. Having to shower in a strange place every day would be a bigger problem.

I suggested that because there is a gap where the walls of the shower overlap the base and there was such a small amount of water on the floor, maybe some water was ending up in the base then finding its way out when the coach moved. I thought the first, easiest thing to try would be to silicone that gap. Ohhhh, nooooooo. That would be too easy to try the simplest thing first. Joe started yesterday by crawling into the bay of the coach, unscrewing three-quarters of the access panel in the floor under the shower and then discovering he couldn't get to the last side of the panel without removing the tire. Problem there. Then he proceeded to remove the drain from the shower, which I will grant you, had been obviously removed and redone at some point, so I guess he had a good idea. After cleaning that all out we needed to make a trip to the store for silicone and plumber's putty. In the meantime, I brilliantly pointed out a number I had seen for RV repairs here locally. Keep in mind that we still hadn't gone with the option of trying to just silicone the gap in the shower wall…OK. Joe decides to call the guy. So the guy was supposed to be here yesterday afternoon by three. It gets to be five o'clock and he calls to see if he can come today instead, he is running late (no kidding). He'll be here between seven and eight a.m. Groan….that means I had to be up and dressed this morning. Bummer.

Anyway, we ended up going out last night to get supplies and grab a bite to eat. Joe wanted to try "Church's Chicken". Their ads made the chicken look pretty darn good. Oh, well. First, the menu threw me for a loop. I could not figure out what came with what for what price. The nice young man behind the counter was very soft spoken and obviously an "English as second language" speaker, so I gave up asking questions and opted for the chicken strips, those being a known quantity.

The meal was the chicken, mashed potatoes (made from the dry flakes stuff), biscuit and included a drink. I took our cups to get myself an iced tea and a cola for Joe while he waited for our order. Not wanting to spill these drinks that were approximately the size of a gallon thermos, I decided to put tops on, which was a good plan until

I pressed down on the second cup and the entire contents spilled out and went into a trash receptacle that was right on the bar with the drinks, straws, napkins etc. Nuts. I refilled the cup with cola, got the lid on safely this time and joined Joe at our table. I told him if I didn't eat some vegetables soon I was pretty sure I'd get scurvy or something, but the chicken looked pretty good and the potatoes, while disappointing, were nice and hot. I opened the container of dipping sauce for my chicken strips and instead of barbeque, honey, or even ranch; I believe there was white gravy with possibly jalapenos in it. Anyway, it was hot and hot. Hmmm. Alrighty then, that was different. On to the biscuit. I didn't see any honey or butter, so I asked a staff person about it and she replied that the butter and honey were already on the biscuit. Upon closer examination it did appear that the biscuit might have been quickly dipped into or rolled in something...possibly butter. At that point I took a big drink of my refreshing iced tea. Only it wasn't iced tea. It was the soft drink. Seems that when I had dumped the one drink, thinking it was Joe's, in fact it was my tea, so now we had two soft drinks and no iced tea. We are not going to discuss the calorie count on this meal, but suffice to say that my fat jeans are now at their limit.

Anyway, we did get our supplies last night and the guy did show up about 9 a.m. this morning, so I'm sitting over at the laundry while they do whatever...there was a lot of head scratching, looking into the bay of the motor home and discussion when I left. Whatever happens I can guarantee it will be expensive.

But, it's not snowing!

Joe is Vindicated!

Although I am still pretty sure we need to reseal the shower wall inside, Joe and our new friend, Danny the RV repair guy, found the problem with the shower leak. Turned out Danny is in the RV directly across from us, which is why the sign advertising his services was on the front of his motor home. Duh. The two of them spent a good part of yesterday taking apart the motor home and putting it back together. Turns out that the p trap (whatever that is) was loose. Usually this is not a problem, however in a motor home it sort of requires that you take apart about half of the coach to get to it. And of course, Joe just needed a new gasket, not an entire trap thingy, but noooo – the only place that even had it would not sell the gasket separately. So that means a 98 cent gasket costs $17.00. Luckily, Joe spotted one under the counter that a customer had taken out of the package, and he got it for only $7.00, a veritable bargain considering what taking the RV into a dealer would have cost.

I am now happily showering in the privacy of my own motor home. Yesterday other than going to the showers here at the park, I spent a total veg out day reading half of a John Grisham novel, eating cookies and watching TV. As I munched cookies, I contemplated the things I like about Texas.

First of all, on January 31st - sitting outside in 79 degree weather. There are flowers blooming. I walked by a tree that was flowering with the most exquisite scent – then I noticed little limes were growing amongst the leaves and flowers. How cool is that? Trees with fruit and flowers in the middle of the winter? I like it. Other good things? There is a Dairy Queen on about every corner. The Mexican food is great. Even chain grocery stores have Mexican specialties. We've had some delicious cheese; also some yummy cookies that are called Royal Assortment. At least that's what I think it says and since I'm the one reading the Spanish label I'm saying it is. The coastal areas are varied and beautiful. There are so many RV parks in the Rio Grande Valley that there is something for everyone. If you enjoy birding and nature, the Great Coastal Birding Trail offers wonderful parks and sanctuaries. If you enjoy square dancing, entertainment, Branson-style shows, again the Rio Grande Valley has all kinds of things to do. The larger cities like Houston have excellent museums, zoos and cultural attractions. But there is one overwhelming plus that outranks all other considerations: NO SNOW! I just went for a walk without a jacket, boots, muffler, furry hat, mittens, double socks or earmuffs. I like it!!

But at the same time, although I have not been in Texas long enough to be an expert on all things Texan, however I am beginning to piece together a few things:

Do you know why Texas women do 'big hair'? Between the wind (everywhere) and the humidity (by the coast) the only way to have any kind of hair style is to tease, backcomb and spray hair within an inch of its life.

Why do Texans wear cowboy hats? Same reason the women do the 'big hair'.

Why do Texans wear cowboy boots? Because they have fire ants and seventeen varieties of venomous snakes running around here. Plus alligators if you get over near the Louisiana border.

Did you know Texans (and I suppose visitors) are allowed to eat armadillos? The wildlife service advises that you may not kill an armadillo for food; all armadillos must be hit and killed by a vehicle or have "died from natural causes". Seriously.

Texans on the environment: there are "Adopt A Highway" signs here, but from the tons of litter it looks to me like most of these poor highways are still orphans. I asked a checkout person at Walmart about availability of recycling for our plastic and aluminum cans, since there is no deposit and return. She had no idea what I was talking about. From the smell and taste of the water I am guessing no one is terribly concerned about water quality, either.

"Live free": Apparently in Texas the idea of zoning is a foreign concept. It appears that anyone with boards and nails can build a structure to live in (or for your goats to live in). There are absolute mansions with falling apart trailer homes right next door and houses that can't possibly be more than 600 square feet. Our motor coach is probably bigger than half the homes we've seen. The other half of the homes – well you could fit this entire RV park into many of them and still have room to throw a barbeque. Most of them are gated....seems prudent.

The Alamo is a much smaller building than you would think. Not everything is bigger in Texas.

All the shops that sell fresh seafood also sell bait. Think about it.

There may be more cattle in Texas than people; it looks that way. And yet the price of beef is about twice as high as Michigan. No wonder so many people here go fishing!

South Padre Island Festival

Somewhere I came across information about a two day Kite Festival coming up on the weekend at South Padre Island. The weather looked less than promising but we decided that since the weather forecasters here are wrong almost as much as in Michigan, we'd go for it.

We got a little earlier start than usual, before 10 a.m. On the way we once again found ourselves wound up in a parade. That seems to happen to us about once per trip. This time we had to avoid the horses but other than that we just sat in completely stopped traffic in both directions for about an hour. The good news was that we stopped right in front of Abby's Bakery. Turns out Abby is a little girl about 3 years old and her father named the bakery for her when he struck out on his own from the bakery about two blocks away where he had been the baker but not owner. Their son was manning the counter and watching his baby sister. I would guess he was about 16 years older than the younger child and I don't know how many others were in between. The bakery did not offer the things we usually see. The Mexican specialties were light, delightful cookies, sweet rolls and the 'empanadas'. Yum, yum, yum. We each took two cookies and two rolls. What a bargain at $2.50. After our stop for treats we probably sat back in traffic for another 20 minutes but we were in a much better mood.

We rolled across the beautiful, swooping causeway from Port Isabel to South Padre Island around noon, making our way cautiously as the yellow lights were flashing, warning us to "watch for pelicans". Saw lights, didn't see pelicans. Anyway, we made the Chamber of Commerce Visitors Center our first stop and then took the highway north towards the Convention Center where the Kite Fest was already underway. We had come through some pretty heavy rain on the way but on the island it was clear and bright with the amazing, colorful kites against a blue, blue sky. We sat in our Jeep watching the kites while we ate our picnic lunch. Then we hiked out to where an incredible variety of unusual kites were flying and being launched. My favorite part was the aerial displays of kites flying in patterns set to music. I've never seen anything like it. We also enjoyed walking along the sand. The beaches are much prettier here than farther north on the coast. We spent most of the afternoon watching the kites and walking, and then finished our trip with a drive out to the end of the island and of course, a stop at one of the gazillion T-shirt shops. We could just imagine how mobbed it must be during Spring Break.

We stopped at the Port Isabel lighthouse and thought we'd explore a few shops when the rain started up again, this time with some pretty impressive lightening. The only other stop we made was for some fresh shrimp – yes, I finally found a place to buy fresh seafood! We were too full from lunch to go out for the seafood dinner we had planned so we put our shrimp into the cooler and made our way back to Mission in a pouring rain. There has been such a terrible drought that one town here has had to truck in water to fill its town water tank since the municipal well went dry. So, I guess we had to be happy for the people that live here but it sort of put a damper on our evening. One of the nice things about RVing though, is that you can just go home and eat leftovers. Oh, and Abby's bakery was open late as we returned back so we stopped in for a few more selections and a couple of breakfast rolls for Sunday morning, so it wasn't likely we'd starve.

Men, Women and the Shopping Gene

Joe and I have a theory about why it is that little girls are carefully perusing the choices, fingering materials and saying, "Oh, cute!" as soon as they are big enough to ride in a shopping cart. Boys in the same situation are either bored, ticked off or playing with something totally unrelated to shopping. We are pretty sure it is hard wired in before birth. Most guys are not into the shopping "experience".

Today was a real test of retirement living as a couple. We spent the day at the Rio Grande Valley Premium Outlets, shopping. Now, I am talking about *shopping*, not the usual foray that Joe accompanies me on...the " hunt it down and kill it" where we go after something, get it, pay for it and go home. Or at the very worst, I load Joe up with coupons and send him trotting around the grocery store to keep him out of my hair while I look around. No, today we did "girl shopping". I'm talking about the real thing – browsing, looking, getting ideas, comparing prices. No specific list, no preplanned agenda, just 'shopping'. Men have a hard time with the concept of looking at things that you may or may not buy (unless the item is on wheels-THAT guys can do endlessly). Even more confusing to them is looking at items you have no intention of buying, for example: a $500.00 Coach purse on sale for $375.00 or a cocktail dress that requires dropping 42 pounds before it could be seriously considered. Needless to say, I had a great time and I actually bought two things. We were there for five hours. Joe was a real trooper although I could see he was totally baffled.

Here is another baffling thing: on the highways I have absolutely no sense of direction. Your best bet is if I say turn left, you turn right instead. Joe has that Italian Amerigo Vespucci gene and just instinctively knows where to go. In a shopping situation it is totally reversed. He has no sense of where we are at all. Case in point- he couldn't remember where he parked the car. We started off in one direction although I tried to tell him we were going the wrong way. We went to the wrong lot and the Jeep was definitely not there. We went back into the Mall and I followed my landmarks. We turned left at the Apostrophe went straight towards Starbucks, made another left that took us by my base point landmark-the Nestle cookie stand. By going out that door we ended up in the right parking lot. Of course, once we were outdoors again I no idea where the Jeep was parked, but no problem. Naturally Joe found it.

After the Mall we went in search of authentic Mexican pottery. Joe didn't even flinch. I think this retirement travel thing is going to work out fine. By the way, it was 80 degrees today with sun and occasional clouds. It is really hard to remember this is February. It was a great day to go shopping.

A Caracara? What??

We spent an interesting day at the World Birding Headquarters. Not sure exactly what I thought, but I didn't realize that World Birding Center is actually nine different locations around the Rio Grande Valley. The Bensten location is actually right at the end of the street our RV Park is on. If you go any farther, the Border Patrol will be asking you questions, or you'll fall into the Rio Grande, or both.

The park is really well thought out with feeding stations, water features and habitats that attracts various birds. The 664 acre preserve has easy to follow paved areas and trails that can be biked or walked. We saw some amazing birds to add to our life list: a Crested Caracara, a Green Jay, a Kiskadee and a whole flock of Chachalacas.

We decided to rent bikes, partly for the fun of it and partly because of my problem with balance and breaking things (like bones), we wanted to see if I could manage a bike. This was a perfect opportunity since they offered 3 wheel 'trikes' for rent. They cost a little more than traditional two-wheelers, but Joe pointed out it would be the most entertainment he's ever had for $8.50. First of all I had trouble getting on the seat, but of course the 3 wheeler wasn't really adjusted for me so that was probably it. Once in the seat I carefully began pedaling and promptly headed for the bushes. I had the handlebars straight but since they were bent at an angle, straight meant right off the road. We walked my trike back and tried another. Much better! Only, my feet were zooming around as if I were taking a spinning class. Joe pointed out that I had it in such a low gear that I had to pedal like mad to move. I adjusted into "2" and zigzagged my way down the slight hill from the Visitors Center onto the path. At this point I thought all I had injured was my dignity but from the number of bruises I had collected apparently that wasn't all.

After that, things went along pretty uneventfully. We got off and on a couple of times to observe at various feeding stations then decided to take the 1.4 mile footpath to the roadrunner habitat. Joe started off at a brisk pace while I was still disentangling myself from my trike. As I caught up with him, he motioned for me to be quiet. There in the path was a bobcat. In my experience, it is a good thing to leave wild animals alone and be on your way. Joe however, thought we should just go ahead and that the cat would be more afraid of us than we were of him (ha-not likely). I backed off but Joe went on, so I trotted along the path to catch up with him while chastising myself for being so silly. As we rounded a bend in the path, there was Mr. Bobcat putting the kibosh on the 'who was more afraid of whom'. Joe beckoned me to come ahead and I started to, but then I remembered that about ten years ago I had discovered that Joe did not actually know everything. I thought to myself, wait a minute…who is Joe? Marlin Freakin' Perkins? I decided to go back to the bike rack and smacked Joe in the back before I hustled off, which was my endearing way of letting Joe know that I was bailing on him. Reluctantly he followed me back to the bike rack.

Joe kept telling people all day that he saw the bobcat. One guy said he had seen it that morning catching a bird. Another guy complained that everybody got to see the bobcat and he had been there five times and still hadn't seen it. One lady mentioned there had been a family of bobcats this spring and how cute the little ones were. The Park ranger assured us that they've had bobcats in the park for the five years she has been there and there has never been any aggression from the animals towards humans.

Ok, ok, ok. I still contend a wild animal is, well, a wild animal and they probably don't like you walking right up to them. And I do concede that the big cat might possibly have been considerably smaller than he looked to me. But I'm pretty sure he could have been fierce if he wanted to…

Turns out we were probably in a lot more danger from humans than anything in the wilderness. While I was dodging the bobcat, there was a gun fight in broad daylight right across the border from Brownsville. In a weird twist, not only were guns blazing in the streets, but there was also a tiger-napping. While I was worried about a tiny bobcat, one of the drug cartels apparently engineered the theft of a tiger from a Circus that had been in Matamoros that day. In the midst of the gun battle, someone stole the Siberian tiger. You have to wonder how they managed that. Here, kitty, kitty, kitty??

Not so funny is that there are apparently no safe places to be in Mexico here near the border. We've been considering going to the one place we've been told is ok: Progresso. Our park managers go there for dental work, prescriptions and shopping. Last night there was the murder of a missionary couple just over the border and a report on a man who disappeared three weeks ago, his truck last seen on camera crossing the bridge into Mexico. I'm thinking we don't really need to go to Mexico.

We didn't realize our RV Park here was so close to the Rio Grande. There is a constant presence of Border Patrol here and today we saw the helicopters scanning the river. A number of folks who have been coming here for some time tell us there has never been a problem here and that being in a gated park adds security so they feel safe. Only two blocks away there is an abandoned house with the windows broken out and obvious vandalism. There is gang graffiti everywhere here. In the same block with the empty house there are two housing developments that are totally upscale homes, probably in the $700,000 to million plus prices. Weird.

And somewhere, a circus is missing its tiger...

The Search for the Elusive Road Runner and More

This morning we went back to Bensten Birding Park because this was supposed to be the best weather day of the week. We planned to get the pass and spend the morning at Bensten and then use our pass at a second State Park for the afternoon. Turns out Mondays the park office is closed. No pass, no gift shop, no guided tours. We decided to make the best of it and take the trail out to the area where we hoped to see the roadrunners. There was not one living thing. No scratching sounds in the brush, not a cheep, a peep, a chirp - nothing. It was basically a nice 1.4 mile walk but no birds. I realize that wild things are not circus animals or pets but geez; we thought we'd see something! (Although the bobcat probably heard about my plan to whack him with a stick, so he wasn't about to show himself).

Since the birding day was out, we returned to the RV to make new plans. I gave Joe a haircut and we caught the Pony Express propane delivery guy so we could get a fill without having to take the coach to the facility. While Joe was showering off two months' worth of hair trimmings I decided to close my eyes for a few minutes. An hour and a half later when I woke up it was a little late to go to Salineno where great birding was supposed to be worth the trip.

We decided to have dinner out. We found the nearest Dairy Queen and used my BOGO coupon for two Blizzards. Hey, we're grown-ups! We can have for ice cream for dinner if we want! Then we went out looking for a few things I had on my list. We've been looking for a juicer. We've seen oranges sold out of the back of trucks everywhere, cheap! and so we had to pick up a bag. The oranges are wonderfully sweet but not so great for eating – better for juicing. One thing we don't have is a juicer. We had already checked two different Walmart but no luck. One had a rack for juicers but it was empty. The other didn't have any, period. So we tried a local chain market, H-E-B and they had housewares but no juicers. Now, we are not looking for a $150.00 heavy duty electric model. We just wanted a little hand held manual thingy to squeeze juice. We tried another Walmart with no luck. At last we found a K-mart. The associates there were really helpful but-nope. At least the guy at K-mart could see the irony that here we are in the Citrus capitol of the U.S. and we can't find anything to make juice. He mentioned that there was actually a grapefruit juice plant right next to where we were shopping. We can't believe that right here in our RV Park are orange, grapefruit, lemon and lime trees full of fruit just there for the picking and we can't find a juicer!

The hunt continues...

Texas Travels Continue

Today we made our way west to Salineno where we had been told there was excellent birding. The town was very, very small but had at least two speed bumps on every single street. We drove up and down every inch of the place and finally found the sign for the birding site. It wasn't what we had expected as most of the birding sites encompass hundreds of acres. This was basically two and a half acres with one area where all types of bird food are placed out several times a day. We weren't disappointed because although we didn't see a brown jay, we did see three different types of orioles. Actually, at one point all three were at the feeders at the same time. We also saw some other birds we hadn't seen before, so it was all good. There was also a path down to the banks of the Rio Grande where you could observe the wildlife there, under the watchful eyes of the Border Patrol, of course.

We got to see a little different Texas terrain on our way west. The flat, flat, flat gave way to some rolling hill country. And yet, still the same weird juxtaposition of beautiful homes next to scrap metal yards, next to goats in the front yard, and even better yet – goats and horses tied up next to the four lane highway and grazing within a stone's throw of the vehicles whizzing by. On our way to South Padre Island we had seen a guy selling German Sheppard puppies out of the trunk of his car. I thought that was pretty strange but today we saw stacks of cages next to a guy's pickup truck with all kinds of birds – green and bright yellow parrot-like birds and multicolored birds. He was just sitting there, waiting for someone to stop on a 60 mile an hour four lane road and buy a bird. I don't know, but somehow I've just never thought of a bird or puppy as an impulse purchase, like you're just driving along and suddenly go, "Oh, there's a German Sheppard puppy in a car trunk, I think I'll stop and get one", but maybe that's just me.

For lunch we chose a little local place in Roma that looked pretty good. Once we stepped in and looked at the menu we realized it was totally in Spanish. Hey, you can't fool us! I called upon my high school Spanish and gamely asked, "Que es numero tres?" My accent must have been totally hopeless because the lady behind the counter mentally rolled her eyes and said something to the manager that apparently meant, "Hey, lucky – this one's for you." He explained that the menu was spiced rotisserie chicken served different ways. We opted for the white meat portion served with the traditional sides: mashed potatoes, rice and tortillas. Again, we will not discuss the calorie count. I've never had a meal with carbs, carbs and a side of carbs.

Today in Texas Started with a Bang

– a bang of thunder that is. Luckily the heavy rain sorted itself out early on and the rest of the day was overcast with just off and on drizzle. But, it's not snowing.

We spent the day in McAllen. Of course, this area is so totally built up that you really can't tell where Mission ends and McAllen starts. At any rate, we were on a quest. The search for the elusive juicer resumed. Also, we had a new lead on where to see the green parrots…and we were off! Although, not very fast because we decided to try a few stores on the way to nail down that juicer. Our 5# bag of oranges wasn't getting any younger. We tried a Dollar Tree where we were told that "sometimes we get those in, sometimes we don't". It was 'don't'. While Joe stood in line there, I went a few doors down to Kohl's. This set a new record. I was actually in Kohl's store and didn't buy ANYTHING! Most notably I didn't buy a juicer because there weren't any. Our last shot was Target and success!! We paid $12.98 for a hand held, manual, plastic juicer to squeeze $4.00 worth of oranges.

Buoyed by our success, we headed for our day's destination: The McAllen Museum of Art and Science. It only took us about an hour and a half to make the half hour drive, because once again we got lost. Stupid GPS. The museum was small but nice and surprisingly well thought out. We ended up at the gift shop and got into a conversation with one of the women there who was originally from Houston. She recommended that we not miss old downtown McAllen, which she described as being like a trip into Mexico without leaving the U.S. Sounded like fun, so after another hour of being totally lost again, we finally found the downtown area and, amazingly – a parking spot. To tell the truth, we only found it because we stopped at the Chamber of Commerce to get directions. The very nice young man there pointed across the parking lot – we were one street off the main shopping area. Oh well.

Ok, downtown McAllen was unlike anything I've ever seen-store after store full of unbelievably fancy, frilly, wildly colorful evening gowns and accessories. The rest of the stores were jewelry, perfume or handbags. Wall after wall, case after case, rack after rack of shiny, shimmery, over the top costume jewelry and the most unbelievable selection of purses. And hooker shoes in every color and style imaginable. The only more amazing stuff was the lingerie....and I'm not going to even talk about that. Not a piece of Mexican pottery anywhere. Nada. Ditto the Green Parrots. Every time I thought I might have seen one, nope – it was either a Pigeon or a Blackbird.

The gift shop gal had also recommended a place to eat where something like a thousand Green Parrots come in to roost at the end of the day. The restaurant was absolutely freezing cold and within six minutes I started to get a headache. While we waited and waited and waited for our tea and coffee we both decided nothing on the limited menu looked that appealing. Since our beverages hadn't appeared, we asked to cancel our order and we left before the full throttle head throbbing set it. Even Joe's nose was cold. And guess what? NO parrots. I 'm beginning to think the locals are messing with our heads.

Green Parrots!

When we checked into Americana RV Park, we specifically asked about the green parrots that we had heard come to this park almost daily. The answer was pretty off hand that the parrots are here morning and evening 'up front'. That was about as much of a nailed down answer as we could get. Naturally, I was not up at dawn looking for parrots or anything else, but we did watch most evenings. We kept meeting people who told us where to see the parrots. One lady told us an intersection in McAllen that has thousands of green parrots perched there all the time. Another told us a neighborhood where the green parrots hang out all day. Not only did we NOT find the parrots, we didn't even find the neighborhood!

We finally decided the green parrot thing was like an urban legend. One bird book stated that all the wild green parrots here are descended from escaped captive birds. We met an avid birder who told us the birds are actually green parakeets, not parrots. Everyone else we met called them parrots. Since we had yet to see as much as a green feather, we figured this was just a way to mess with the heads of those of us who visit the RGV. It had gotten to be a running joke with us every time we saw a flock of birds…"was that a parrot?"

Yesterday was just a terrific day. The sun came out first thing in the morning and the rain finally shopped. Seems like it has rained off and on the whole time we've been here. The drought was much worse than we "northerners" realized, so I can't begrudge the rain for these folks but wow! It was great to see the sunshine.

Joe was enjoying his coffee when he called to me, "Oh, my gosh! It's the green parrots; come over here quick." Sure. I was going to believe that. But he was insistent and when I looked I could hardly believe my eyes. A flock of large, brilliant green birds swooped as one unit right by our window. They came to rest and eat the berries from a tree two lots down from us and stayed for about half an hour.

We had great opportunities to view them with the field glasses, watch their antics and take pictures. The sun on their nearly iridescent feathers was just fantastic. They did exist!!

Full disclosure: This picture taken on our 2nd trip to Texas.

Crapper's Full…

Well, we had a great day yesterday with the green parrot sighting in the morning and ending with a really good dinner at Texas Roadhouse. Ironic, we finally got a good steak in Texas at a nationwide chain restaurant. We got the motor home pretty much ready to roll and battened down so that all we had to do in the morning was to wash up breakfast dishes and bring in the slides, unhook and be off. Even though the day was rainy and gloomy, the green parrots came back this morning to give us a sendoff. It seemed like a good omen.

We were bringing in the bedroom slide when my cell rang. I almost let it go to voicemail but luckily I decided to get it even though Joe was shouting at me that the slide was only half way in. The call was from the RV Park we were heading to in Corpus Christi, wondering where we were. Seems our reservations were for Saturday and now it is Sunday, uh oh. I have so much trouble with the last day here/first day there being the same day. I've just been waiting to goof up and here it was. Fortunately, they were holding a spot for us and giving us the full two week reservation. Whew!

While I was wondering how I got off by a day, Joe was busy with a hard core toilet cleaning tactic. One of the challenges of RVing is keeping things smelling, shall we say, 'fresh'. Fussy me…always complaining that the toilet just wasn't working properly. So a quick check of the internet led me to a number of suggestions for cleaning, using some rather interesting equipment. Joe emptied the gray water tank and black water tank, and then flushed the black water tank again. The method called for dumping a couple bags of ice and a quarter cup of dishwashing detergent down the toilet. Supposedly, while the coach is on the road, the ice sloshes around and cleans the tank, then the ice melts and everything is clean. Things seemed to be going ok with the first few pounds of ice, then suddenly the ice stopped going down and the ice was clogging the entire toilet. Uh, oh. After breaking the toilet brush and discovering that toilet brushes are not good ice picks we decided to just hope it would melt. Joe dumped in a couple of buckets of water but unfortunately most of it ended up on the floor. I grabbed a stack of cleaning rags and a roll of paper towels and jumped into the cleanup. Joe cheerfully reminded me that it could have been worse – this was CLEAN water. Of course by then I absolutely, positively had to use the bathroom again before we left, so I trotted off to the Park ladies' room. By the time I got back, Joe had already pulled out the Jeep, which was supposed to be my job. Between the two of us, a few more trips back into the coach and some dirty looks from a couple park residents while we were blocking the road, we were almost ready to pull out. Then we discovered we had totally forgotten to put the braking system in the Jeep before we cut off the power. Rats.

I had hoped to get a picture of the green parrots but by the time we finally redid the Brake Buddy and I was able to get my camera – you guessed it – they flew off. It wouldn't have been so annoying except for the fact that I accidently wiped the SD card and the copies on my computer the night before so, no pictures of green parrots, or anything since Galveston for that matter. I know, I know…I'm the one who is so paranoid about losing pictures that I always keep all of them on the card as well as on the computer. Worst of all, I have no idea how I did it, so I don't know how to keep from doing it again! Ackkkk. Everybody tells me how easy these photo programs are so easy to use. Well, apparently not for me!

So, finally we were on the road, hopefully ice and detergent sloshing away in the black water tank; the GPS lady seemed to have lost her recent grudge and it was all systems go-until we had to stop. The Border Patrol checkpoint was pulling over everyone, including old people in RVs. Traffic crawled along 3 lanes wide as the officers, sniffer dogs and surveillance cameras went over each vehicle. However, when we finally got to our turn, the officer asked if we were US citizens (yes) and if there were any other passengers in the RV (no). That was it. I think we could have had five families of illegals stuffed under the bed and breezed on through. Not that I am complaining! We lost about 25 minutes as it was and luckily the Border Patrol isn't looking for nonfunctional tail lights, because that we *were* guilty of. Somehow in hooking up the Jeep, between my unscheduled trip to the bathroom and putting everything together twice, we didn't leave enough slack on the line for the plug that supplies power to the Jeep while in towing mode. That wouldn't have been a real problem except when the plug got pulled out it was totally chewed up beyond repair so it was useless to try to plug it back in. With electricity not running into the car, the braking system wasn't working, or the lights. For once I was soooo glad that Texas is very flat. The motor coach brakes will stop the car adequately without the braking system, but not necessarily on hills or at high speed.

Joe left extra car lengths between vehicles and made good, hard braking stops. Maybe those firmly braked stops were a good thing. At least, something finally worked because I went into the bathroom and gave a tentative flush even though the ice was still clearly visible up into the bowl. Ka-woooosh... We had never heard the commode make a noise like that! All the ice went shooting down into the depths and now the toilet works better than it ever has since we bought the coach. I think the Flamingo Express had digestive problems. Well, I think we have it solved now (I hope) and all we need to do is go buy a new toilet brush and a new electrical plug and I think we're back in business! I guess we'll find out when we leave here in two weeks and head for San Antonio.

Chapter 7

Good News

Joe was able to find a replacement plug for our electrical connection and amazingly, our friend George had brought a tester with him to Corpus Christi (only a retired electrician would do that, but lucky for us.) Between the two of them they got it fixed and we now have turn signals, lights and brake lights again. The toilet is flushing like a trooper and we figured out how to hook up the cable TV. We now have 158 channels. Of course about a 100 of them are in Spanish, but still we have something like 55 more channels than we need. Things are looking pretty good.

I thought our park would be right on the water but apparently a drainage ditch is about the closest water we're going to see here. Luckily, the condo our friends rented here is on the Gulf, so I think we'll be inviting ourselves to their place a lot. We met to plan our week and went out for lunch together at a place I picked. Boy, they were good sports. It was a very small place and not very appealing from the outside. I have been in Texas for a month and have yet to sink my teeth into some barbequed brisket. It is practically the official state food and we haven't gotten even close to barbeque so I was determined to try the first place we could find featuring barbeque. Inside wasn't very impressive either, but boy, the food was good and well-priced. I was glad that one of our forays into a local, hometown, hole in the wall restaurants was good since we had George and Carol with us.

We went our separate ways after spending a few more minutes finalizing our plans here at the RV, then Joe and I headed to the H-E-B store (kind of like our Meijer, only with a whole lot more Mexican foods). As we were going in we met George and Carol coming out! I guess they won't be able to escape from us!

We finally found some decent looking steaks. In the Rio Grande Valley we just didn't see any good meat at all. Hard to believe in a state that raises cattle you can't get a good piece of beef. Anyway, George told us he'd gotten some good New York strip steaks so we looked for those and picked up a package. I guess the only way we're going to have a good steak will be to cook it ourselves. It took us forever to pick up a few items mainly because the store was laid out like no other grocery I've ever seen and the shoppers run their shopping carts like they drive....no apparent pattern, stop and go, driving down the middle of the lane. I think Texans are some of the worst drivers in the nation. We've been cut off so many times I've lost count. Horns blast, drivers zoom around you, then slow down or change lanes in front of you only to make a turn immediately afterwards. If we can survive the traffic, the shopping and our own screw ups, we'll be headed home a month from now.

February 23, 2012

We have a couple more days here in Corpus Christi before heading up to San Antonio. Here at Colonial del Rey we ended up being a long way from the shore, but that wasn't all bad. It has been nice and quiet here, which we enjoy. And although the sign says there is "Absolutely NO repairs to be made in Park", Joe decided that didn't mean minor repairs. The windshield wiper had worked loose and was no longer making the entire sweep of the humongous front window on the driver's side. Everyone told us to bring a ladder, so we didn't bring a ladder. Joe enlisted my help to move the picnic table at our site. Of course, I couldn't even pick up the corner of it, so he ended up dragging it around to the front of the bus. Not tall enough. He decided to take our little round ottoman out, put it on the picnic table then balance on that. I suggested that might be a bad idea. We compromised on: picnic table with a one step stool on top. So, Joe got up there and discovered he didn't have a wrench big enough to fix it. Off to Home Depot. By the time he got the wiper working properly it was getting late, so we decided we should enjoy the rest of the day. We hadn't been to the old downtown of Corpus Christi, so once again we braved the freeway and headed downtown.

The downtown area features some specialty stores and restaurants but the hands down best place was The Blue Frog Mercantile. What a fun place! All kinds of interesting and unusual things from children's clothes to artwork to melt in your mouth fudge. We spent most of the afternoon there.

The other area of Corpus (as the locals call it) is a lovely collection of early 1900's homes that have been moved to "Old Irishtown". The Art Museum, Visitor Center, Museum of History are all clustered together in the same area as the historic homes. I wish the houses were open for tours, but they all have a plaque telling about the home, its owners and history. We returned to our RV Park by way of the road that runs right along the Gulf. Talk about lifestyles of the rich and famous! Most of South Shore Drive/Ocean Boulevard is just one amazing home after the next. My favorite looked like a life size sand castle. We decided to go back the next day and see the area a little more.

Ash Wednesday was a nice day again, high 60's and sunny. We headed back to the shoreline drive. We were just as impressed as we had been before. Corpus Christi is unusual in that after the 1909 hurricane the seawall that was built to protect the city was actually made with steps so that residents could go down to the water. The mooring areas that are built in a "T" are called T heads (no brainer, huh?) and several downtown streets end up at the T heads on the water. We mooched around looking at boats and soaking up the sun. It was so hard to remember it was February. On our way back we stopped at a small park hoping for a bit of a walk to stretch our legs. What an unexpected gem! The unassuming looking little city park opened up to a boardwalk out into the wetlands and then the bay where we saw the most ducks and shorebirds I have ever seen. It was amazing. We saw three birds we had never seen before. Ok, maybe not as exciting as the Green Parrots, but still…

Wednesday evening we went to the church right down the street from us where we had gone on the weekend. There had been a Lenten fish fry, so how could we pass that up? We met some nice folks there who had sold their home and become full timers. I can't believe how many people give up their home base and live in an RV full time. Again, my "stuff" needs a place to live!

The Ash Wednesday service was at 7 p.m. and the pastor asked if anyone had failed to observe the Lenten fast and abstinence and had eaten a hamburger…there was sort of a hush and the pastor boomed out in a hearty voice, "You're gonna burn!!" The entire congregation cracked up laughing. It appears that today's Catholics have realized we are not one cheeseburger away from eternal damnation. Thank God.

The church was absolutely packed. I always marvel at American Catholics. You can't drag more than a handful of us to a Holy Day of Obligation, but a day like Ash Wednesday that seems to be very meaningful to us; well, we pack 'em in, obligation or not.

Today was predicted to be hot, hot, hot, 85 degrees in Corpus, high 70's on the Island. Seemed like a perfect day to go out to Padre Island National Seashore again. Our friends George and Carol came over from their condo and we all piled in the Jeep, lightly dressed and slathered with sunscreen. The fog was supposed to lift around 11:30, so we figured the sun would be out by the time we hit the island. Nay, not so. The temperature struggled up to about 70 but the fog never totally dissipated. The sea, sky and surroundings stubbornly remained gray all day. We sat in on a very interesting program by a Park Service Volunteer as part of their "Presentations on the Deck ". She talked about the Gulf currents and all the stuff that washes up on the beaches. There are an amazing number of weird, scary and interesting things that end up on the shore. Next time you buy something in a plastic bottle, remember that believe it or not, it can end up in the ocean and kill an endangered Sea Turtle.

We took a short (3/4 mile) hike into the interior of the island and then went to "Doc's" where we enjoyed a terrific seafood late lunch while overlooking the bay. Topping off the day, we stopped at the German bakery again to introduce George and Carol to the delights of strudel, and did the quintessential "tourist" thing - go to a t-shirt shop, where we actually found some really cool stuff. Ah, yes…More "stuff". .See why I can't live in an RV full time?

This is not a McDonalds…

We enjoy visiting churches in different areas as we travel. The kind of cool thing about the Catholic Church is that no matter where you go it's always the same even though it is different. The order of the service, the rites and prayers of the church are comfortingly familiar even if the music, the building and some of the local traditions may differ.

When we visited the local parish in Mission, Texas we got a warm welcome. Texas hospitality met us at the door with the greeters who offered a firm handshake. Inside the place was packed. A courteous gentleman insisted that Joe take the seat he vacated for him.

There were so many large families of five, six and seven children! Many extended families were present with obvious fondness between the generations. A youth group presented the music with exuberance and singing was enthusiastic. It was heartwarming to see a church so alive and connecting with all ages. Maybe that is why we were a bit taken back to come across a copy of the church "rules". I can't remember all of them or the exact wording but the tone was clear. This was a CHURCH! Those attending were reminded this was not the golf course or the beach - no tank tops, shorts etc., please. There was something to remind participants that this is a house of prayer. And the best part – here I paraphrase, but it went like this- "If you are expecting to be entertained, served coffee or looking for the drive through for McDonalds…you are in the wrong place." I chuckled but I had to give them credit. Here are people who know what they are about and what their mission is, with no ifs, ands or buts. This is a place to worship God, be in His presence and commune with other Christians.

In Corpus Christi we found we were camped only about two blocks from the Catholic Church. By the time we were there it was Lent and oh, boy…Fish fry! We queued up on a Friday night with the locals and wow! What a crowd. We figured it must be good. The guys in the kitchen were hustling and fish was frying, flying out the door and for eating in. Homemade pies and other desserts were lined up on the side table. Despite the heat and the hustle, everyone in the kitchen was cheerful and upbeat. Joe walked back to compliment the guys on their food and he was given a hearty invitation to come back the next week. Boy, we wished we were going to be in Corpus another week!

Almost Time to Move On

We spent yesterday going to the Fulton Mansion in the Rockport area and apparently it was a very exciting trip because last night I had a hard time getting to sleep. I spent a few hours on the couch, then tried to quietly get back into bed but of course, I woke up Joe. I must have felt terribly guilty because I pulled the covers over my head and woke up at 10:30 a.m.! Whoa – I couldn't believe it was that late. This is a new personal best for me – I did not get dressed until 12:30. Boy, a day goes by really, really fast when you sleep through half of it.

We got it together to go to H-E-B and Walmart to pick up a few things before we pull out tomorrow for San Antonio. As usual, we know it's about time to move on because we finally know our way around the city pretty well now. By the time we ran errands and made it to 5:00 p.m. church service, had a snack and cleaned up the RV for going on the road tomorrow another day was pretty much done.

Back to the trip to Rockport: we got to the mansion just in time to miss the noon tour. Boy, these people are serious about tours! The front and back doors are all locked up until each tour begins, and then the back door is unlocked and you are ushered out to the porch at the end. (**And** they lock the door behind you). The wind was blowing off the water and right through our jackets, so we decided to look around the area until the next tour. The 1 p.m. tour started promptly, so it was a good thing we had come back and were waiting to get in before they locked the door again. Interestingly, the state of Texas spent a million + to buy and restore a number of historic homes in Texas then made them state parks. I think they needed to set aside a little more money. The roof on the Fulton mansion is leaking and only two floors have been restored for tours. The house itself was quite amazing; built in the 1800's with indoor plumbing and central heating! The owner had been a bridge builder and had the place built to be capable of withstanding a number of hurricanes over the decades. The smartest thing he did though was to marry the daughter of his employer. The daughter then inherited 28,000 acres of Texas grazing land. Not bad. Long story short, that's how he ended up in Texas and rich enough to build a mansion.

Anyway, I attempted to be on my best behavior and not break anything as well as try to redeem myself for firing off my big mouth the day before. We had gone to Padre Island National Seashore again but with George and Carol this time. Joe was just really interested in the Volunteers there who do various jobs and stay at the VIP RV camp. While he went in to talk to the lady who had done the presentation we had just seen, I confided in Carol and George that I had an uncomfortable feeling Joe was trying to get me back to work. Believe it or not, Joe came back out with a brochure on Volunteer work camping and he proposed we look into it. My immediate response was, "Bite me". George and Carol nearly fell off their seats laughing. It's not like I planned to say that. I just reacted and probably because I had just *said* that Joe was plotting to find me employment. They were still laughing off and on all day. Well, you can't say I don't give an honest reaction. I keep telling him I've finally found what I am really, really good at doing: nothing! I just seem to have a knack for it. Oh, and one other thing too. Shopping. Saw the perfect sign yesterday: Money can't buy happiness - that's what shopping is for! Well said.

Chapter 8

On the Road Again

Well, I'll say one thing for the parts of Texas that we've seen so far: nobody is going to sneak up on you! Most of the areas have been flat, flat, flat. If some hombre gets the drop on you, must be you just weren't paying attention.

So we are headed to San Antonio which is in the "hill country". It will be interesting to see how much different it is. Like Michigan, or most states for that matter, the weather, the land and the people vary from one region to another. We just passed miles and miles of refineries and related industry after leaving Corpus Christi. I would think that pollution would be a big concern here. And I can now see why refinery fires are so horrible. There is so much 'stuff', storage facilities, electrical wiring and substations, all crammed in close together.

Speaking of pollution, we sat in on an interesting presentation at the Padre Island National Seashore. It was all about the things that wash up on the beach. I have to say it was somewhat disillusioning. I had a mental picture of the National seashore as pristine white sand, billowing foam, lines of waves washing onto the shore forming little tide pools and washing up gorgeous shells, yours for the taking. Not so much. Because of the Gulf currents and the way they converge on the Texas coast, all kinds of junk ends up there-animal, vegetable and Dr. Pepper vending machines. I just can't imagine how a vending machine gets into the ocean, floats for hundreds of miles and washes up pretty much intact. That was just one of many strange and weird objects that wash up all the time. The Park employees and volunteers clean several miles of the beach daily, but the restricted area of about another 60 miles is only cleaned up periodically. Visitors are asked if they would like a plastic bag for picking up trash as they walk the shore. We were warned to watch out for medical waste and drums of unknown substances. Yikes. Most amazing to me is that the National Park has all this stuff just piling up in a heap there on the island. No one is recycling it, investigating for toxins or leaking barrels, not even hauling away the scrap metal for cash. Is that nuts or what? Still I have to say that the staff works hard to keep the beaches cleaned. It was an enjoyable place to walk along the waves even if there were a considerable number of croaked fish and on our previous visit, all the dead Man o' War. The facilities there are very well done with good educational exhibits and programs.

It is hard to believe man could completely pollute something as vast as the ocean, but I think we are giving it a good try. We saw warning signs on a number of beaches about entering the water or eating the fish due to the pollution. Most people seemed to be fishing with a total lack of concern about any warnings. Probably the same mind set as fishermen in Michigan who proudly proclaim that they have been eating fish out of the Great Lakes all their lives several times a week and nothing bad has happened to them. We can only hope that turns out to be true.

San Antonio

Everyone we have met who has been to San Antonio has told us we would love it. Now we know why. It is really a unique city and a wonderful place to visit. Only we weren't too sure we were going to make it. A few blocks before the RV Park where we had reservations was the worst railroad crossing I have ever seen. It was built up at something like a 90 degree angle, no kidding. Joe hit the brakes and crawled over as easily as he could but I think it was miraculous that we didn't lose the undercarriage of the Jeep or tear something off the coach. A limousine would get hung up and see saw back and forth like a teeter totter. We pulled into the park with a real feeling of relief, only to find the office closed due to their RV Park Olympics being in full swing. Luckily a resident helped us out and we were headed towards our spot which required navigating a hairpin turn and then backing into a space that had no kidding-less than 10 inches on either side. Joe got it on the first try – you go, Joe!!!

So our site overlooked San Antonio River which was great except the river was barely a trickle and an addition to the Riverwalk was being worked on right behind us - not so good. The next morning we awoke to two caterpillar tractors running right outside our window. At least there was more water in the river and a few happy ducks were paddling around oblivious of the workers running all over the banks. The RV Park had advertised that it featured eight miles of trails at their site, connecting the Park to the historic Missions. Well, the new Riverwalk extension resulted in the closure of the trail. And because the new trail wasn't open yet there was no walking to the Missions from our location. I have to say that the Riverwalk is so terrific that it will all be worthwhile because you'll be able to go all the way into downtown or out to the Missions when it is finished. We'll just have to come back!

Where's the Sunshine?

There are 300+ days of sunshine in San Antonio yearly so naturally it has been raining since we've been here. Most of the activities here are outdoors so we are hoping for some dry days before we leave. We did go out to find the Visitors Center yesterday. It was a little tricky because I have three different guide books and all of them listed a different address for the San Antonio Visitors Center. We found it on the first try but there was no parking for twenty blocks in any direction. So, I hopped out and Joe went off to circle the block. Actually Joe ended up about five miles away so good thing we had our cell phones otherwise we might not have ever seen each other again.

I was happy to make it to the Visitors Center before they closed. Unfortunately I don't think the staff was that thrilled to still be at work. I thought I asked POLITELY about where we could find parking downtown. She looked at me as if I had just asked directions to the Alien Space Landing Site.

"There is parking all over." she informed me.

I was stammering trying to pose a clearer question about where and how expensive the parking might be. Again, we failed to communicate. Fortunately, I had seen a sign about free parking on Tuesdays, the 'free parking pass Tuesday'. So, I asked if you have to be like, regularly parking downtown, like daily or something, to get the free Tuesday. Wrong question. After another rather hopeless interchange I finally asked where I could get the pass for free parking Tuesday. Turns out there is no pass. It's more like: we'll give you a pass on having to pay for parking. By this time the staff person was totally sure I was a complete idiot. So this morning we went on the web to see if we could figure out where the parking lots were. I ended up calling about parking and was told that the commercial parking (which I had called) has nothing to do with the city parking.

Sheesh. I finally got a hold of the city and found out that Tuesday parking in any city lot is indeed FREE – yay!! But only after 5 p.m. - boooo.

Here's a very good thing: the RV Park here is quite nice and really *is* right on the river. Well, sort of – technically it is the river but right now it's more like the "creek". Actually, the area right outside our coach window is going to be really, really nice when completed. The city of San Antonio is extending the river walk by several miles and the landscaping and the improvements are well underway by this section of the river. It looks like it will be lovely.

Hopefully tomorrow will be a better day for sightseeing. We've gotten a handle on how the city is laid out and we managed to salvage today with a tour of the charming historic home district and yummy, yummy barbeque brisket for dinner. I love it when Joe cooks (which includes taking me out for dinner). We stocked up the pantry, wine cellar (the 2nd bay on the passenger side of the coach) and fridge, so hopefully if the weather cooperates, our friends George and Carol will be here and we'll make another run at enjoying the sights of the city.

On Monday, February 27 we took a sort of "overview" tour of the historic homes area. The historic district is laid out so that you can see many homes on a walking tour. I recommend that you go to the Visitors Center (closed on Mondays) in the district for a brochure that will tell you about the homes. At least one home is open for tours. The sheer number of magnificent restored homes and surrounding gardens is just amazing. We also discovered there is free 2 hour and in some areas, unlimited parking in the Historic district. Take that - $10 dollar parking!! So, we took the short flight of steps down to the Riverwalk and followed it to the center of town. It was an enjoyable half - mile walk in an idyllic setting.

The following day our friends joined us and we returned to the Historic District with a driving tour, then parked in our free parking spot (score!) and took the Riverwalk to the Alamo. Putting it that way makes it sound like we just hoofed it right to the Alamo. Ohhhhhh nooo. That would be too easy. Although the walk is well marked, somehow we missed the best place to walk up from the river and get to the Alamo. And, although I take water with me EVERYWHERE when I walk, guess what? Forgot water. The temperature crept higher, the sun got hotter (oh, sure NOW the sun shines) and I could feel myself turning shades of fuchsia. I finally told everyone I needed water, a bathroom and a cool place to sit down until my blood pressure was somewhere in the realm of normal.

We finally asked directions and ended up in the Riverwalk Mall where I cooled off a little and we found the "shortcut" to the Alamo. We were pretty late in the day but I was so glad we got inside. Spoiler alert – I'm going to ruin it for you if you haven't been there, but the Alamo was really not what I had expected at all. The Alamo was right smack downtown. I had pictured it surrounded by open land and a tranquil, respectful setting. Instead it was right across from

Ripley's Believe It or Not, a house of horrors, an IMAX theatre and just swarming with people. Once inside, it was much more than I expected. Extensive work and restoration has been done to make it educational and an appropriately fitting memorial to the men who died there. We walked back to the Jeep and headed out to dinner at Rosario's, a Zagat rated Tex-Mex restaurant with wonderful food. I think we all felt we had burned off enough calories to deserve it.

The next day: road trip. It's like the old story about three blind men describing an elephant – Texas is not all flat and filled with scrub; we just hadn't seen much else. The Hill Country rolls and dips and has larger trees and lusher looking fields. It was a beautiful drive and we had perfect timing, getting to the Natural Bridges Cave just in time for the next tour. If you have been to the Mammoth Caves this would be a bit of a letdown perhaps, but it was a very interesting tour with some beautiful formations and bonus! - a really nice gift shop. We returned to San Antonio; the guys threw some steaks on the grill and we ate outside on the picnic table. A soak in the hot tub and swim in the pool made a nice ending to a lovely day.

The Hill Country of Texas

We decided to go to Fredericksburg, a Hill Country historic community with lovely restaurants and little shops. We fueled up with a big breakfast at the Mexican place across the street from the RV Park. Observation: although thousands of people start their day with beans I personally do not recommend it. After making the rounds of the three other Missions in town, we hit the road.

Once at our destination, we started at the Visitors Center at the Chamber of Commerce, and then headed to the Visitors Center on the main street. Kind of crazy – two Visitors Centers in one little town. We took the tour of historic buildings and learned about the largely German settlement of Fredericksburg. One interesting note-still surviving are a number of "Sunday Houses". The far flung ranchers would come to town for Saturday shopping and stay for Sunday church services. They built one room bungalows just for their weekend stays in town. I've never seen that anywhere else.

We then found the best pie shop! Their pies had been featured in Taste of Home and Southern Living. George tried to charm the recipe for the Orange Brandy Pecan Pie out of the staff but no luck. We decided we'll have a bake off and taste testing when we get home and just keep making pies until we get it right. The guys went to the beautifully done Nimitz World War II Museum and we girls hit the blocks and blocks of shopping. What fun places! It's a good thing we ran it out of time before we ran out of money!

Friday it was back to just Joe and me and since his museum pass was still good for the day, we decided to drive back to Fredericksburg. It was kind of a long drive, but what the heck? We're retired!

Joe left me and the Jeep downtown and he headed back to the Museum. I still didn't make it through all the shops but I sure tried!

We finished our day at one of the several German restaurants in town and had a relaxing dinner. We drove back into San Antonio at night and it is a beautiful skyline, day or night.

By Saturday we were almost out of time to enjoy the city. My top two choices were to have a boat ride on the river and lunch on the Riverwalk outside under an umbrella. We headed back one last time to our free parking spot and walked to the Riverwalk shopping and dining area. Rain had been forecast earlier in the week, but the day was picture perfect, clear and bright and a little cool. We arrived at the main ticketing area just in time to sit in the boat and relax a few minutes before taking the narrated tour of the river. I think our guide was a little hung over but he did a really good job. After our ride we chose Casa Rio, the restaurant you always see on picture postcards of the Riverwalk with the colorful umbrellas. The food was outstanding. Boy, if you can't find good food in this town you just aren't trying. It was absolutely perfect and a memory to last forever....well, at least Saturday morning and lunch were. Then it was back to reality as we lugged ten days' worth of clothes to the Laundromat to wash then get ready to pack up to roll out on Sunday morning. I could have had another week in San Antonio with no problem.

No wonder everyone assured us we would love San Antonio!

Chorizo – It's Not Just for Breakfast Anymore.

We have always enjoyed trying local foods and getting into the local cuisine. The grocery stores in most of the areas we have visited in Texas carry a popular sausage that is quite different: chorizo. It looks very spicy but it is not really as hot as it looks-but that's only because it looks **blazing** hot. Joe really wanted to try using some in a traditional dish: chorizo and eggs. We looked at one package after another, reading labels. I nixed the one containing 'beef salivary glands'. I'll interject a thought-now I'm really wondering exactly what is in all kinds of sausage. Ick. Anyway, we settled on a brand that seemed to have more appetizing ingredients but at a medium price.

The package suggested one sausage for each egg, then remove the casing and brown carefully being sure to cook fully. Joe decided maybe that was a little much for starting out. He went with half a sausage and two eggs. Just cooking the sausage was a trip. Getting the sausage out of the casing was a messy process and the contents contained a number of mysterious looking things. It appeared to have kernels of corn; we later decided that must not have been it, because the cooked product didn't have anything that remotely resembled corn. The sausage cooked down to about half grease and half meat. Getting the grease drained was a two person project as we tried to avoid pouring any grease down the drain. Joe got the eggs beaten up, cooked the whole thing together and it wasn't too bad. It was much better if you didn't spend time thinking about what might have been in it.

Well, that left us with two and a half more sausages. Joe suggested that this stuff could make great tacos or burritos. So, now it was my turn to deal with the chorizo prep. I tried draining and then using paper towels to dry off the most of the grease. I combined it with about 4 ounces of hamburger, added a teeny bit of taco seasoning and made up some flour tortillas with tomatoes, lettuce, cheese and a little salsa. Not bad! I'm embarrassed to waste food, but I have to admit we ended up throwing some of it out. Word of warning: you may want to try chorizos in dishes other than eggs, but DO NOT let this stuff spoil. You hardly think it could spoil with all the peppers and whatever else, but when it does…oh, boy. Holy buckets! Trust me; you just don't want that to happen in your refrigerator.

Chapter 9

The Day Lana Accidentally Drowned the Mouse

Well, here we are in the 'wilderness' adventure part of our trip outside of Austin. I picked the Bastrop River RV Park partly because it was a very highly rated KOA and Woodall's' 10-10-9 rating and partly because I didn't want to be in a big city like Austin. Situated right on the Colorado River but only 1.3 miles from the highway, I figured this would be the best of all worlds. Uh, oh. Sometimes things just aren't what they seem. First of all; the Colorado River isn't **the** Colorado River. We were kind of confused about how the Colorado would run into Texas. This Colorado River is in Texas because it should have been named something else. The conjecture is that a map maker just accidently mislabeled it. Unlike the various towns, counties and destinations here that have been renamed, the Colorado River remains. So, here we are on its banks - although not exactly the setting we had in mind. When I saw we'd be over a mile from where we got off the highway I didn't realize we were going to be going 1.3 miles exactly parallel to the highway. Or to be more specific, there are two, 2 lane service roads and a four lane highway with in throwing distance from our park. As the trucks roll by and the cars zoom past day and night it's not exactly what I had pictured. Luckily the train whistle breaks up the highway sounds periodically.

Then there is the nearby town of Bastrop. When planning our trip I had not realized that about one-third of the town had burned down with the recent wildfires. So, I guess the good thing is that the historic section was spared. Then there is the rest of the bad news. The "Lost Pines" were a landmark we planned to see. Note I said 'planned to see'. This venerable stand of old growth pine that mysteriously grew up near Bastrop all burned to the ground.

Then there is Baron de Bastrop. Streets are named after Bastrop, as well as this county and city. The Baron was a notable Texan who was a friend of Sam Houston. The Baron turned out not to be nobility at all, but a runaway tax official from Holland who was accused of embezzlement. Despite that people here in Texas seem to totally overlook the guy's background. Bastrop, Texas was originally named Mina but apparently no one is rushing to change the name back in view of the facts that finally came to light in the last century.

Well, we have managed to do it again. Since probably 25 years ago when we accidentally went to New Orleans the weekend of Jazz Fest and couldn't find a motel room for 100 miles, I seem to end up in places with 500,000 extra people in town when I want to be there. Luckily we were able to change our San Antonio reservations so that we avoided being there for Rodeo with 1.5 million other visitors-no kidding-that was the estimated number reported for Rodeo. Yikes. The Riverwalk was probably more like the River "crush". So, despite my best efforts, checking websites, gathering Visitor's Guides and reading books on the area, here we are again. Turns out this weekend is the South by Southwest Festival in Austin, whatever that is. It is expected to draw 200,000+ people. Double Yikes. So today we are heading to Austin in the hopes of avoiding all the crowds. Local TV interviewed Austin residents who were leaving town for the weekend because they know there will be no place to park or any chance of getting seated at a restaurant. So, it's Tuesday and Austin, Texas. Once the traffic picked up we were awake early anyway so we got up and running. Or should I say up and spilling? Somehow when I put two boxes of cereal on the table, one knocked over the second one, which knocked over my very full coffee cup which spilled coffee all over the table, bench seat, computer and the wireless mouse. Poor mouse. I have the batteries out and left the cover off, but I am afraid it is dead. Time will tell. Then somehow it took us three tries to get ourselves in the Jeep and on the road. Maybe that's why Joe didn't want to take time to pull in the awning this morning. I made mention that the wind was picking up and maybe we should roll it up but ever the eternal optimist, Joe said, "Naw, it'll be fine." But more about that later.

It took us over half an hour to find the Visitors Center in downtown Austin. We actually did find it once, but thought it was a tourist trap trying to trade on the name "Visitors Center" but it turned out the 'trap' was the place. Finally armed with brochures and information on parking, we headed to the Texas State Capitol building. It was worth the trip. The beautifully restored and refurbished Capitol is amazing. We took advantage of the free tour and then wandered around on our own for a time. We decided to have lunch in the cafeteria where we could rub elbows with the movers and shakers. That is, if they were there moving and shaking… The Texas legislature only meets for 40 days in two years. They receive about $7000.00 a year for their part time job. I think they may be on to something here. Maybe the key to having fewer stupid laws is to keep the House and Senate out of session as much as possible. We queued up and grabbed a tray. The food looked pretty good and quite reasonable. Oh boy! More brisket! I asked for the brisket plate with two sides. The server slapped a spoonful of some chopped up meat with barbeque sauce on my plate. "Excuse me" I asked, "is this the brisket"? The server replied in heavily accented English that it was "chopped beef" – at least I think that's what she said. It didn't *look* like brisket but it tasted ok.

Fortified with lunch we took on the Capitol Visitors Center which is in the old Land Records building and has a very nice staff, exhibits and a movie. From there we finished up the day by driving around in circles looking for the Historic District to do the walking tour. I have this real problem. If I am not holding the map the same direction as the streets I can't tell where I am. Finally Joe pulled over and took the map. Turned out we were where we needed to be to start the tour. And more amazing, we even found a parking spot!

Austin's motto is "keep Austin weird". We found it a little weirder than our comfort level. After wrapping up our tour of the historic highlights, we headed back to the RV with one short side trip to photograph yet another giant squirrel. Who would think there would be two in the state of Texas? But then, everything is bigger in Texas. As we headed towards Bastrop the wind continued to pick up. I kept thinking about the awning. We pulled in and–Relief!–the awning was still intact. As Joe struggled to get it rolled in, the neighbor came over and told him that they had been worried the awning would tear off in the winds today. They felt uncomfortable bringing it in as they have found some people really get upset if someone messes with their RV. We thanked them and established a new rule: If you don't need it out, roll it up.

And one happy thing to end the day–the mouse has resurrected from the dead! I put the battery back in and we are clickin' away. Yes!!

Day in which Joe Gets an Armadillo

We decided to spend another day in Austin. I didn't really think there was that much else I was interested in seeing and since this South by Southwest thing started the next day I wasn't too keen on the traffic and crowds. Actually, I think traffic around all the major areas of Texas is bad so it probably didn't matter that an extra 200,000 people were coming into town. Any thought we might have ever had that we could not pull a car and just drive the motor home wherever we wanted to go was really, really stupid. Anyway, we decided to make it LBJ day.

We started with the Lady Bird Johnson Wildflower Gardens. As usual, we got a little lost but finally found it. The weather had not been spectacular and I didn't expect much so early in the spring but what a nice surprise! Many flowers, bushes and trees were in bloom. The gardens were very well done with several water features and excellent examples of native plants. There was also a nice little café so we had a cup of soup and a hibiscus mint tea. It was like sitting in a screened in porch at a friend's house. With that, we went out to the trails even though the weather was looking a bit iffy. One trail featured open land, one more wooded. I felt better in the woods because I figured we were no longer the tallest thing there in case of lightning strike.

Anyway, the rain held off until we had done both trails and we headed into the Gift Show as it began to shower again. This was a wonderful gift shop with many lovely items. But what caught my eye was a little stuffed armadillo about 10" long and looking quite like he would anticipate riding in a motor home. I slid him under my arm with my purse and furtively scooted up to the register. I softly asked the clerk if she could quickly bag my armadillo (haha – I asked her to bag an armadillo, that's kinda' funny) and not let my husband see it. She probably thought this was a bit strange but she got right into the spirit of the conspiracy, popped the little guy into a brown bag and rang up my purchase. For some reason Joe didn't ask what I bought. May be he was too shell shocked from the blazing speed at which my VISA was being used on this trip but for whatever reason, he didn't seem to notice. When we got back to the motor home I tucked the armadillo under the bedspread with just its little face sticking out. I was going to put it on the pillow under the covers, but I was a little bit concerned I might give Joe a heart attack. But more about that later.

After the Gardens we went to the LBJ Library. It was not exactly what I had pictured but then what usually is? The price was right – free and free PARKING! It was nicely done although a new gift shop is under construction (bummer) but my VISA card got a chance to cool down. The views from Lady Bird's office overlooking Austin were terrific. That inspired us to trek over to the highest point in Austin which is reached by rounding a breathtaking number of hairpin curves and ridiculously steep grades until an area for parking levels out. Ok, what Joe didn't tell me was that there were 734 steps to the top. Although I was panting at every landing it was worth getting to the top. What a panoramic view of the river, the city and miles and miles beyond! We spent some time at the top while I wondered what was under the ledge that the observation area was on and watched as people climbed outside the railing to get a better look at a zillion feet straight down. It's a wonder the human race has survived this long. It threatened to rain again, so luckily going down is much easier than climbing up.

Since it looked like rain the rest of the day and we weren't especially hungry, we decided to go back to the RV Park, have a snack and pass on eating dinner in one of Austin's great restaurants. That was probably a good idea as not only were there crowds coming in for the festival but also a local icon passed away and a downtown vigil/remembrance was planned. It was BYOB&T – bring your own boa and tiara. Leslie was a street person who ran for Mayor of Austin three times. He was a cross dresser who was known for his fondness for boas, tiaras and thongs. His own line of specialty refrigerator magnets featuring his flamboyant outfits and let's say 'interesting' poses was apparently his main source of income. Well, what with the vigil for Leslie and all, it seemed like a good time to head back to home base.

When we got back, as I said, I managed to pop the armadillo into bed without Joe noticing it so I sort of hung out reading until he went in to go to bed. I heard him laughing and not bludgeoning a poor helpless armadillo, so I knew he had found our new little passenger and realized he wasn't a threat.

"Where and when did you get this?"

I couldn't believe I actually got one over on Joe – he always notices everything while I'm living in my own head oblivious to my surroundings. I'd say the armadillo and I had the last laugh. The little guy now rides shotgun with Joe by the driver's seat of the Flamingo Express and whether he likes it or not is hard to say. But I'd guess any armadillo would rather be on the bus than under it.

Sometimes Things Just Go Right

We decided that since the weather forecast wasn't looking great, we would make another run at finding the hiking trails that go along the Colorado River. Here we go again….the GPS tried taking down a through street that didn't go through and from there we just drove and drove. Sometimes you just trip over things that are better than what you looking for in the first place. We ended up on a dead end in a Business Park where an art foundry was located with their showroom next door. Wow! The place rivals some of the finest Art Galleries we've seen. The only hold up was that everything was out of our price range…way, way out. But it was amazing to see.

Luckily we soon stumbled upon the entrance to the river trail not far away. The trail started out pretty level but as we got towards the river bank it became much steeper and narrower. Pretty soon we were scrabbling up and sliding down like a couple of elderly mountain goats. As the trail became narrower it also branched off in different directions. Periodically I looked back to get a mental picture of how the trail would look returning and made careful note of the turns we took. It was left, left, left and then a final right. Although, on the way back it sort of seemed like it might have been left, left, right, right. Hmmm. Not good. Then it started to rain. Uh oh. It looked like it was going to rain harder and by then we had arrived at a split in the trail to go on to another trail section or go back up to the road and hopefully turn in the right direction to get to our vehicle. We decided to retrace our trail through the woods since we didn't really know how far it would be on the road. The rain was light and all was going well until I noticed that nothing looked familiar…and it started to rain harder. About the same time, Joe told me he didn't think we had gone this way….uh oh, again. So, I had violated one cardinal rule of hiking; I didn't bring a map. And guess how many bars I had on my cell phone? Uh, none. Joe had me stay on the trail while he hiked back in the opposite direction to see if we had made a wrong turn. As

I was standing there remembering all the wisdom about what not to do when you are lost in the woods, Joe came trotting back and waved me on up the hill. Of course, by then I was totally baffled as to which left, left, left and right were now, left, right, right and right. The "going up" turned out to be a little bit more challenging than the going down had been. Finally, panting and puffing, wet on the outside and very dry on the inside we were really, really happy to see the Jeep. And since the road ahead of us was totally washed out preventing traffic from going on further, it was pretty easy to find our way back out of the area. Live and learn.

One really outstanding moment of the hike was when we came to a clearing that was full of Texas bluebonnets in full bloom. It was like a special gift…the bluebonnets aren't even supposed to be in bloom for another month. Then on the drive from Bastrop to Smithville, it was just one big display of wildflowers.

Yesterday we were on a quest to see the Lost Pines. We found out that the Loblolly Pine (seriously) did survive in the State Park next to Bastrop State Park, so we headed for Smithville and the park entrance. When we got to the entrance of the Buescher State Park, we found out that only about six miles of the park was open. It seems that after recent wildfires had decimated both parks, two weeks ago they got a nearly unprecedented amount of rain. Needless to say that following a drought the ground was so dry that most of the roads washed out. Fire, flood-what's next? Plague of locusts? These people can't catch a break. However, on the road entering the park was a nice stand of the Loblolly (Lost Pines). They are magnificent for Texas I guess but compared to Michigan pine trees the poor things look a bit scruffy. With so little of the park open we figured just driving up to it was enough. That turned out to be pretty good because we then took a tour of 'historic' Smithville. Yes, yet another 'historic' Texas town. Actually Smithville is pretty cool. It has so many old homes, storefronts and scenic spots that something like nine movies have been made there, including Hope Floats, with Sandra Bullock. Smithville was the hub of the railroad system before the turn of the century (the 20th not the 21st). At one time the town boasted of eight hotels and five grocery stores. With the end of the steam locomotive, Smithville's fortunes took a downturn. But in recent years they have reinvented themselves. We stopped at the Visitor's Center which is housed in the old train depot and boasts a giant gingerbread cookie in the park next door. Smithville is also in the Guinness Book of Records for baking the world's biggest gingerbread man. (I presume it has been eaten by now, the one in the park is made of wood).

We had a delightful visit with the woman at the Visitor's Center who also recently had her first grandchild. She told us all about the film industry, the history of the railroad line and the recent fire. I think it was probably Joe's charm, but she gave us a very nice soft side cooler and two bottles of the locally bottled rainwater in biodegradable and recyclable bottles. Cool.

After taking a tour of the historic homes we got in the Jeep and headed back to Bastrop where we made a last stop at the Texas Boot Company. I never knew there could be so many cowboy (cowgirl?) boots! I picked up the first pair because they were pink and cute-but like $400.00! Uh, that is my shoe budget for the next six years. Joe kept saying I should buy a pair. The salesperson, who was wearing a cowboy hat and looked to be about sixteen years old, was very polite but I think he had us pegged for greenhorns who were never going to buy a pair of $500.00 boots. Even the "work" boots were big bucks. But that didn't come close to the hats. Honest truth - we saw a Stetson that was behind glass with a $1000.00 price tag. For that price I hope they come to your house and custom fit it on your head. I guess the only boots we'll be buying any time soon will be winter, waterproof and in Michigan.

–Ode to the Armadillo

Where Art Thou Texas Armadillo?

We have looked both high and low

But haven't seen an armadillo

Thought they'd be like possum are

Along the road or whacked by car

The only one that we _did_ see

Was drinking beer in an eatery

We visited a thousand miles

All throughout the Texas wilds

Don't put a chocolate on my pillow

Just show me the armadillo!

There's just one thing we want to know

Where'd the armadillo go?

(…and I haven't seen a rattlesnake either, but that's OK)

Chapter 10

The Road Home March 10, 2012

We are headed back to Michigan by way of Nacogdoches, Texas where the Azalea Festival starts today. I planned our route to catch the azaleas in bloom but I figure it will probably be like our trip to see the dogwood in bloom on the Natchez Trace years ago. When we got there one lonely little dogwood flower was barely clinging to the branch of a single tree out of miles and miles of dogwoods. Or like our usual timing for the Holland Tulip Festival. We've been there for the "bud" festival and the "stem" festival but usually miss the actual tulips. Timing is everything.

We've had sort of a depressing drive so far. Acres and acres of scorched land, burned houses and dead trees from last year's forest fires stretch out from both sides of the highway as we leave Bastrop. These folks will come back though. We saw so many posters, bumper stickers, billboards and people wearing t-shirts with messages of support and optimism. It's just sad to see all the devastation. We learned from one of the locals that the fire was probably much worse because the Texas Horned Toad (I am not kidding-like Yosemite Sam's "great Horney Toads") is found in Bastrop State Park and to preserve its habitat the parks service did not do 'prescribed burns' to help keep the underbrush cleared. So with the tremendous drought and all the fuel for the fire, it was just horrific. I have a sneaking suspicion the toads are toast.

Yesterday we had a really nice day although it rained for most of it. We took a day trip to San Marcos which is a college town, home to Texas University. We didn't really expect it to be such a big town so once again we drove around lost for a good part of the day. I am getting somewhat disillusioned with the GPS. Sometimes she doesn't seem to have a clue where we are. And it would also be helpful if she understood the words "Visitor's Center". We finally did find the San Marcos River falls and even in the rain it was very scenic. By then we had accidentally driven though the historic district so that was enjoyable. The highlight of the day was the boringly named, "Dicks Car Museum". I had to sort of talk Joe into going; he didn't really expect much. Wow, what a surprise. This place was beautifully done, exceptionally clean, well lit, well displayed and had some of the most fabulous cars we've ever seen. We spent almost three hours there and could have stayed longer. The classic cars are all models before 1959, in absolutely pristine condition and displayed with information about each. I think Joe may have taken a picture of every one!

We are ignoring our GPS lady and taking another route, so I guess that makes me the GPS lady. I think I'd better pay some attention to the map so Joe thinks I can actually read it and get us where we are going. I'll let you know how that turns out.

In Search of the Elusive Azalea

By March most of our great ideas from New Years' eve are long gone. OK, I haven't lost thirty pounds yet but I have been fairly good about my main resolution: make sure to be grateful for something every day. This past Saturday it turned out to be a no-brainer to be thankful for a little blessing of the day.

When we were living in Alabama (if you can call it "living") I remember a woman gushing to me about how we had to go on the "Azalea Trail". Over the years I remarked many times that was a trip I would like to take. Then about twenty years ago I started trying to find out exactly where this "trail" was and when to go. As a matter of fact, Texas, Alabama, Oklahoma and one of the eastern seaboard states all tout their Azalea Festivals. I planned our route back to Michigan from Texas to stop in Nacogdoches, Texas on the first day of their Azalea Festival. As luck would have it, we got off to a late start somehow and with the lousy rain we got into town quite a bit later than I had hoped. We didn't have very good directions and once again Ms. GPS didn't understand "Visitor's Center". We drove onto the historic downtown district's main street and Yay! - There was the Visitor's Center. It was two minutes after four p.m. – guess what time they closed? Four o'clock. The place was locked up tighter than an old lady's one size too small Spanx. Drat.

So, we set the GPS for area parks, thinking that would be a logical place for planting displays. Nooooo. Silly me, I assumed this would be like the Holland, Michigan Tulip Festival with banners displayed, signs marking the 'Azalea Trail'. Uh, not so much. I told Joe we should just drive back downtown and nose around some of the little shops that were still open and maybe find a place for dinner.

We found a parking spot, looked up and there were azaleas in bloom right in front of us. Actually, they were next to the Visitor's Center and somehow we hadn't seen them. Well, at least it wasn't going to be a total loss. I did see SOME azaleas. Across the street, which by the way was paved with bricks and lined with charming store fronts, I spotted a shop that just absolutely called my name. We wandered in and were greeted by the very friendly owner and her beautiful golden retriever. While I shopped, Joe got to talking with the lady about the Festival-or lack of... Turns out she had maps, brochures, directions and the good news that the azaleas were already in bloom. And you wonder why I am not much of a believer in coincidence! Our timing was perfect. The rain had even let up!

We followed the directions to the Stephen F. Austin University grounds and found the gardens. In particular, the Ruby M. Mize Azalea Garden was just amazing. There were over 700 azaleas of different kinds from native to brand new hybrids. The acreage was flooded with pinks, fuchsias, reds, purples, apricot, lavenders and bright whites. Some of the colors were so intense it made my eyes ache. We walked under flowering dogwoods and magnolias and in the shade of loblolly pines viewing the flowers until it was almost dark. As we left the park the rain started again. It was like God had parted the clouds and given this special gift just to me. Of course, then it was back to downpour again, but life is like that isn't it? We can complain about the rain or ignore our wet feet, close our eyes and still see the flowers.

From Armadillos to Azaleas

Wow! I don't think our first big trip could have gone much better. OK, there were a few setbacks, some learning curve involved and a couple of near misses from big storms, but we survived it all. And we didn't kill each other. There is something to be said for that. Some of us got grumpy a couple of times…might have been me. I can't say as I'm really ready to go home yet, but the motor coach bays are too full to cram any more purchases into, so I guess it must be time.

We ended up with our last stop at an RV Park once again right off the highway. It would have been a nice campground except I-57 curved around two-thirds of the sites. That, and there was a train track somewhere nearby because we heard trains about every half hour. And again-the attack of the giant caterpillar. In San Antonio there was earthmoving going on right behind our rig and here again- same thing, except for some reason at this site they began knocking down trees about seven p.m. and worked in the dark. It looked like there were drainage tiles waiting to be installed but who knows? At least we've gotten pretty good at sleeping in all kinds of conditions so the only thing that kept me awake for a while was my throbbing 'this little piggy had roast beef' toe on my right foot.

One kind of odd thing in our motor home is the placement of the electrical outlets. Some of them are really hard to reach. I like to use the laptop at the table but the outlet is way at the back underneath where you can't see it or reach it easily without crawling under the table. I'm sure you are already getting a picture of this that is not pretty. Anyway, yesterday I went to plug in and decided that instead of trying to pretzel myself around the brace for the table on the floor I would just flop down on my belly on the bench seat and plug in the cord from there. Bad idea. I got down ok, I got the plug in ok, but getting back up was a different matter. I was, shall we say, stuck…I tried wriggling backwards but didn't have enough room to push up with my arms as I went. I laid there on my face for a few minutes and finally decided that I would be best to try to propel myself straight backwards as hard as possible, clearing the bench and then stand up. This might have worked well except for the fact that against all odds I rammed my middle toe into the drawer pull on the opposite wall in the process. Owww. The stupid thing looked like a purple Popsicle. Well, that hurt.

So, we're on our way home pretty much intact. I take back what I said about Texas being flat, flat, flat. Parts of it are for sure but there are also hills, piney woods and coastal areas. It's a big state with many different people, ways of life and landscapes. We didn't make it to the desert and Big Bend National Park so I guess those are destinations for another trip. But for now it's blue sky, clear highway and homeward bound.

Return from Texas March 2012

It is so strange to go away for months and after a day or two back at home it feels like you had never been gone. Or is that just me? We are back to our usual meal and cleaning schedule. We dove right back in to doing 'stuff' around the house. We found out that the shingles on our five year old house have failed because they were not put on correctly. Basically the shingles are sliding down the pitch of the roof. The people who made the shingles aren't liable – shingles are fine they were just put on wrong. And the builder went out of business in the recession. The good news is we spent money like we still had it while we were RVing and didn't worry because we didn't know we'd come home to a $$$$ project.

So, in the meantime, the armadillo has found a home perched on a lampshade (I think he's a real party animal). He's going to be a house armadillo until we go on the next trip. The new flamingo plant stand is snuggled up to his big sister in the front yard, waiting for warmer weather. And speaking of warmer weather, Joe and I are both watching our weight again – or yet. I am at a complete loss as to how we could have eaten less and walked, hiked, climbed and otherwise exercised so much on the RV trip and gained weight. I had been really carefully dieting before we went on the road. I lost almost 20 pounds and found 18 of them while we were gone.

I had gotten a new scale with digital readout when I started a new diet plan. No more standing on one foot or weighing three times and taking the best number or leaning until the scale reads in the range I'm looking for-this new one is annoyingly accurate. Imagine my concern when I first stepped on after returning home and the reading said 'error-error-error-error'. I panicked thinking that my new scale didn't even go high enough to register the bulk I am carrying. I tried stepping on again and at least I got the numbers even if I didn't like them.

So Joe and I decided to go on a plan guaranteed to lose 9 pounds in 7 days. All we lost were the 7 days. OK, that's an old joke and we did both lose two pounds so I guess we can't say it didn't work at all. This is so maddening. I did all the easy stuff years ago – no more cream and sugar in my coffee, no butter on anything, no sugary drinks; eat a piece of fruit rather than have a glass of juice, switch to lower calorie everything you can find. Then we started the harder choices: whole grains, brown rice, skim milk (yuk), smaller portions, more fish (double yuk). Why is it that we never wake up in the morning craving a plate of delicious steamed kale? A fresh brewed coffee with flavored creamer, a cinnamon roll slathered with cream cheese frosting, followed by a nice Belgium waffle with strawberries and whipped cream and perhaps a few slices of bacon for a bit of protein....now that makes getting out of bed worthwhile. I'm just saying, why *is* that? Oh well. If I want to be able to climb up the steps to the motor home I'd better stick with it.

Well, the coach is cleaned from vacuumed ceiling to mopped floors and clean carpeting. We're all buttoned up until fall. Spring cleaning is underway throughout the house and the garage and pole building are due for straightening and reorganizing. We have boats to launch, docks to put in, and projects, projects, projects. No chance of being bored until it's time to load up the Flamingo Express for the next adventure. I'm glad to be home but I'm already planning the next trip.

I have had a most disappointing day. Well, not the entire day. I went to lunch with my friend Col and we did a little fun shopping at our favorite places. Ah, the joys of retirement! Before going out I had gotten up early to stir up a batch of sugar cookies so they could chill before baking when I got home later today. Here's the disappointing part.

I had decided to add an extra festive touch to the upcoming weekend dinner by including the "Easter Armadillo". When we were in Fredericksburg, TX there was a great kitchen shop where I found an armadillo shaped cookie cutter. So, as a little surprise for Joe, I thought I'd make armadillo shaped cookies with a creamy brown frosting and a little tiny chocolate chip as their beady little eyes. Unconventional, yes. A good idea, no.

As I rolled and cut the cookies they seemed a little hard to handle. Now this recipe is absolutely yummy and never fails. Of course, when I made the dough I did sort of pick up the wrong measuring cup for the sugar, but I compensated by throwing in more at the end of the mixing process. Anyway, it's hard to imagine I was at fault. I blame it on the armadillos.

They didn't look too bad going into the oven except for a propensity to lose their tails but when I opened the oven – oh, no. Some of them looked like wart hogs, some like buffalo, some like mutant dinosaurs but pretty much none of them looked like armadillos. Disappointing. Then I tried to get the little suckers off the cookie sheets. I went through three different spatulas trying to remove the cookies without totally mangling them. It was pretty sad.

Then, in my quest for the "perfect cookie" I may have eaten a dozen or so, not wanting to have really ugly cookies hanging around.

As a result I think I'm experiencing some sort of diabetic episode which is probably because of my goals for the Lenten season: I decided to work on one of the "Seven Deadly Sins" and gluttony seemed like the most obvious choice. In the spirit of putting on a perfect Easter dinner I had to set aside my Lenten promise and given myself a dispensation to eliminate the bad cookies. I'm sure glad I didn't make 4 cups of brown frosting before the armadillos were baked. I would have had to eat that, too.

For some odd reason, I feel a little queasy. Luckily I have time to recover before our next big trip coming up in the fall. See you on the road!

An Armadillo finds a Home in Michigan

After the long trip from Texas back to Michigan, our new little friend, Beaufort the Armadillo, found himself many happy places to hang out around the house and settled in to a life of leisure. Free from the fear of becoming road kill, he wandered about his new home at will, showing up in many unexpected places. One morning I opened my underwear drawer to find Beaufort peacefully snoozing. Another morning Joe found him perched on top of the hanging clothes on Joe's side of the walk in closet. Under pillows, hanging precariously on lampshades, popping up from under the covers on our bed and even in the bags on the motorcycle – you could never predict where the armadillo might turn up next.

Yes, all was well with Beaufort until a certain, shall we say, 'wanderlust' showed itself in his eyes. One day he was gone! Finally we found him – packed up and ready to go in the motor home! Well, we could hardly blame him for being anxious. You see, by this time we were beginning to wonder ourselves when we'd be leaving.

Our summer plans of entertaining, household painting, cleaning chores and much more took a back seat to other more pressing concerns once we were back in Michigan. All winter I had been looking at Joe's arm with more and more concern. Before leaving last fall he'd gone for his annual checkup and I had specifically asked him to have the doctor look at a mole that I thought was 'not right'. You know how sometimes you can't exactly say what's wrong; something just doesn't seem right? Well, Joe is generally a really healthy guy, works rings around men half his age, lots of energy and strong as an ox, so I know he was pretty sure I just needed something to fret about. For once I didn't go with him to his annual appointment; can't even tell you why, now. Bottom line, he got a clean bill of health and Doc assured him the spot was "nothing". But after looking at it all winter I was more uneasy than ever.

Not usually a big fan of morning TV but one day I happened to be watching one of the news shows and caught an announcement about

"Melanoma May". Free screenings for skin cancer were being offered around the country and viewers were urged to contact a local participating physician. I thought that might be the way to get Joe to a dermatologist – a free appointment. I knew darn well that after he'd been told there was no problem he wasn't going to pay someone to tell him that a second time. But the look of that arm just kept worrying me, so I hopped on the internet to see if I could find someone nearby. I tried several searches and was just thinking better of the whole idea when I got linked to the American Cancer Society. From there I found the only provider in our area who was offering screenings. I called, thinking both Joe and I could go in and get checked out. Well, there was one – only one, appointment left so I made it for Joe. It was three days away so I had to think fast how I was going to talk him into going.

After I made the appointment I told Joe that I wanted only one thing for my birthday this year. No gift, no dinner out, absolutely nothing except one favor: would he keep this appointment that I made for him to see a dermatologist? I did throw in the part about at no charge, hoping that would seal the deal. I could tell he was less than enthusiastic but I could also see that the lure of not having to shop for the wife at birthday time was looking pretty good to him too. He agreed to go.

At his appointment, the doctor had several of his staff come in to look at Joe's arm. You would think that was a clue, but Joe was still sure it was nothing. He was scheduled to have the suspicious area removed in the doctor's office one week later and he came home afterward sporting a huge bandaged lump on his arm. He was more than annoyed and pointed out to me if I didn't like the way his arm looked before, well - this was not exactly an improvement, was it? So while he remained annoyed, I was stoically awaiting bad news. Unfortunately, after shadowing him constantly for a week, I finally went out to lunch with a friend and of course, that's when he got the phone call with the pathology report. Not only was it cancer, it was a malignant melanoma – the deadly type of skin cancer. And to add to it, the surgery didn't get it all; he would have to return for further surgery. After a total of three surgeries, 3 rounds of removing stitches, 3 pathology reports-finally the good news-clear margins, no more cancer cells. The armadillo hung out in the motor home expecting to wrap his tail to a secure spot and get ready to go on down the road. But no, not so fast.

After a quick trip to the cardiologist for a clean bill of health the next stop was the internist for the annual checkup and renewals on routine prescriptions so we could get on our way. During the appointment an unexpected development – a heart murmur that apparently hadn't been there 18 days previously at the cardiologist's. So, as long as we were making the rounds of getting tests done, doc ordered an x-ray to check on Joe's chest since the melanoma often shows up next in the lung. The Medical Center hadn't recommended a follow up x-ray, nor had the local dermatologist but what the heck? Figured we might as well leave no stone unturned.

The heart murmur sort of threw us since it was totally unexpected. Neither one of us thought too much about the x-ray so we were totally taken by surprise when the results came back showing a 9 millimeter nodule in the right lung. WHAT?? Where did that come from? Boy, some days it's enough to make an armadillo cry.

One Happy Armadillo

So, the leaves had been showing off their brilliance and Mother Nature outdid herself in Michigan this year…I guess I'd have to say I'm glad we were here and didn't miss it. After the incredibly dry summer we had I expected the leaves would probably just shrivel up and fall off the trees. But, to our delight, the vivid scarlet and deep burgundy, intense orange and shades of yellows made for the most amazing display we've seen in years.

But as glorious as the fall has been here, I was happy to tell Beaufort the Armadillo to sit down, hang on and shut up because we're taking off! All Joe's further tests proved to be either that something miraculous had happened or the first round of testing wasn't very accurate. Take your pick, but let me just say that I know God answers prayers. Maybe even quiet little prayers whispered by very small armadillo.

So as soon as we pack up and pull out, we'll be on the road again.

Chapter 11

And We're Off - Almost

What a beautiful day to get ready to hit the road! We definitely won the weather lottery with clear, sun filled skies and moderate temperatures. We were scurrying around like squirrels gathering fall nuts-back and forth to the motor home with food, clothes and supplies. It was so nice out that we left the windows open for a good airing of the coach before getting on the road. Yup, things were going swimmingly and packing was going well.

By lunch time today we were down to boiled eggs and pickles left in the refrigerator. We have had some rather weird meals trying to get down to one refrigerator (we turned the extra fridge in the garage off for the winter). Maybe the unbalanced nutrition of late is what caused the mental lapse.

We have a safe in the motor home. I'm not telling you where, but I can assure you that it is very unlikely you can break into it because we have found out we can't. It turned out that neither one of us could remember the combination. We know it isn't part of our social security numbers, our birthdates, our phone number or our house number. What we don't know is what the number IS. And guess where our passports are? Luckily, there is a work around; it can be opened with a key through a port that is hidden on the safe. OK, problem solved. So, Joe says to me, "Where's the key?" You may not be shocked to find out that we couldn't find the key. Well, two hours later we were still trying to figure out how to open this sucker.

So it appears that we won't be leaving yet. Luckily we also found some tortilla chips and a hunk of cheese left so I guess we won't starve. I only hope that nachos are brain food.

And We're Off-Slowly October 18, 2012

We both worked really hard getting everything wrapped up yesterday; turned in our absentee ballots, made sure the insurance was back on for the Flamingo Express to be on the road, packed up last minute items and double checked lists, lined out items on lists, rewrote lists…This morning I finished a final load of laundry, emptied the dishwasher, unplugged the garage refrigerator and made sure we were ready to go. By 9:30 we were looking pretty good. We had decided to wait for the garbage truck because on our one lane drive there is no way a garbage truck/motor home showdown is going to end well.

In other words, we weren't exactly on the fast track to get out of town but all was going well until Joe finally got ready to drain the pipes in the house and discovered that our whole house generator wasn't running. After some discussion about how necessary it was to have the generator available since we weren't leaving the water on, we decided that we really shouldn't go until we got it figured out. Joe tried one fix which resulted in a blown fuse. Ok, off to Plainwell for another fuse. New fuse in, jump start the generator a second time: nothing. It actually had started the first time he jumped it (which apparently made the fuse fail) so we were out of ideas. The company that had installed the generator had been sold but luckily I did remember who bought them out and even more luckily, we were able to get them to agree to come that afternoon. Ok, not an ideal situation but we decided to take off before they came out. Now it was after 11 a.m. but that was ok. We were only about an hour behind schedule.

Not having hooked up the car last night since the garbage truck was coming today, Joe had decided we'd use the local church parking lot to hook up. I drove the Jeep and followed the Flamingo Express as she lumbered down the road. I must say I did a very good job of lining up the tow vehicle so Joe could get the tow bars on while I put the Jeep transmission in neutral very, very carefully-following my written instructions step by step. I don't want to be the one to drop a 4 wheel drive transmission on the ground. Good. We just had to hook up the automatic braking system and pull away. Joe did the install and I watched the test display in the motor home. Uh, oh. Test failed. As a light rain began, Joe went through the whole procedure again. 12:30 and I am really wishing we had decided to eat some breakfast. I know absolutely nothing about how mechanical and electronic things work but I do know two things: 1.This was not a smart time to suggest that Joe should maybe have tried out everything on the motor coach and tow car before the day we were leaving and 2. If you're getting an error message saying there's no signal-uh, maybe there's something not attached that should be. I had sense enough not to get into item #1 but I did cautiously suggest that maybe that doflunky thingy that is on the side of the firewall in the Jeep wasn't attached or something. Joe didn't say much but he trudged back to the Jeep and as I watched the display – Eureka! Test passed, system go. I may not know the right name for a doflunky thingy but apparently if it's not hooked up the system doesn't work.

But have no fear – a few hours later than planned but we were well on the way to Ohio. The sun came out and we enjoyed a fabulous color tour all the way to the Indiana border. It was about there I realized that the eggs I had left in the refrigerator for the breakfast we decided to forego were going to be there when we got back. And about six weeks old. Uck.

Hello Toledo! October 19, 2012

We pulled in to the KOA outside of Toledo, Ohio in pretty good time yesterday despite our late start. The nice folks here took us right to the site and helped us hook up. Another camper immediately came over to Joe and started asking questions about pulling a tow vehicle. They were newbies and it felt good to have somebody ask us questions... last year we were the ones looking for help. Must be we look like we have some clue what we're doing now.

The wooded setting of our camp and the few campers in residence made us feel pretty sure we were in for a nice quiet stay. I had been looking forward to hunting for gems in their mining attraction here. We came by a quarry on the way, so I was pretty excited thinking we were in an area of natural rock and who knew what kind of treasure? Apparently a "Gem Mining Attraction" is a little tiny fake water tower overlooking an oversize sandbox which has been salted with 'fossils' and 'gems'. Or else I guess you can purchase a bag that already has the sand and 'gems' inside. I wasn't that clear which it was, but needless to say, I need some further education regarding how you find gems. First hint: don't look at a campground in Ohio.

Well, life is full of disappointments but at least we got in ahead of the rain, had a nice hot soup dinner and a good night's sleep awaiting us in the peaceful countryside. Once the whistle blew and the not too distant rumble of freight trains began I realized it might not be as peaceful as we had hoped. Funny, we never heard a train during the daylight hours...

In any case, guess we were tired because we both managed to sleep pretty well and get rested up for our explorations in the Toledo area. A good cup of coffee and we'd be rarin' to go! What I had forgotten is that the motor home coffee pot is a bit tricky. You have to get the filter seated exactly right or you end up with the Mount

Vesuvius of coffee pots. Unfortunately we both forgot to keep an eye on it and as a result, we had coffee and coffee grounds pouring over everything. Joe caught it before the floor got soaked and I discovered that the new paper towel dispenser we installed doesn't unroll the towels without a fight, but we sopped up and mopped up and then strained out enough coffee grounds from what coffee did end up in the pot that we each got a cup.

I had planned a day at the zoo but the weather had other ideas. A light steady drizzle turned to off and on soaking rain. Backup plan: Toledo Museum of Art. Wow, what a surprise! I didn't realize the Libbey Glass Factory was in Toledo and that this is a real center for glass. Due to the generosity of the donors, mainly the Libbey family, the Art Museum is an amazing place. The exhibits span over a thousand years and are interestingly arranged by periods and culture. But probably the most outstanding part of the museum was the glassware exhibit. Housed in its own separate building made entirely of glass, including the interior walls, the building was as interesting as the contents.

We were fortunate to catch the 2 p.m. glassblowing demonstration. The extremely talented artist was first and foremost an educator. The Museum has a school for glass blowing and has turned out some really fantastic artists. Would have loved to bring home some examples but the prices were a little out of our reach. On the other hand, the Museum itself was FREE! What a retiree bonus! Absolutely free admission every day. And due to a parking lot renovation that is going on now, the regular $5.00 parking charge? Also FREE! Score! Being Friday the entire facility was open until 10 p.m. and this particular date, a pianist was playing in the Café and other special events were planned throughout the evening.

And I can't forget to mention the Café. Usually institutions have food that is, well, institutional. I'd say Frederick Meijer Gardens in Grand Rapids is one exception to that rule, but now I would have to add the Toledo Museum of Art as a second. The café had a delightful menu of two unusual homemade soups, several salad selections, several sandwich selections and a half sandwich/combo option. Not that impressive you say? Ah, ha – but what amazing choices….for example, Joe had a salmon BLT. Artisan bread toasted and stacked with a generous slice of grilled smoked salmon, bacon, and fat fresh tomato slice, crisp lettuce and an herbed dressing with a beautiful salad on the side. My chicken salad featured the same salad Joe had: crisp greens (no soggy iceberg here), crunchy red grapes, halved baby cherry tomatoes, in handmade vinaigrette, topped with croutons and included a huge portion of grilled chicken. The coffee smelled so good when we walked in and since we were coffee deprived following the exploding coffee pot incident, we each enjoyed a large cup of fresh brew that was as good as it smelled. All this while seated in a three-sided, floor to ceiling glass "courtyard" room with a view. We spent the entire day and could have stayed for the evening if our feet could have taken any more of the hard floors.

We did find our way back to camp. Was there any question of that you say? Uh, well, kind of…I usually pick up a business card at sign in, put it right into my purse and make sure we have an address to find our way back to where we left the motor home. Maybe it was first night on the road, I don't know why, but this time I forgot. Luckily, Joe picked up a copy of the camp rules to take with us in the Jeep because it had a map on the back-and the address. Good thing. It's not convenient to forget where you left your house.

Tomorrow: on to south of Akron. It turns out I didn't mean to end up south of Akron but that's another story…

Well, this was one wild ride through the great state of Ohio. I may have made a slight tactical error in booking our present campsite. We are taking the train through the Cuyahoga National Park tomorrow so I wanted to be near Akron but well situated to continue on to Pennsylvania on Monday. Somehow we have ended up about halfway to West Virginia. In my defense, not a lot of campgrounds are open after Labor Day.

Joe decided to follow the GPS instead of the map I had gotten ready for today. Oh boy. I thought all of Ohio was flat. Turns out not so....there are rolling hills, hairpin turns, near mountain slope grades and that was all BEFORE we hit the detour! I don't really get carsick but by the time we got to Bear Creek I was feeling a little green. Then I stepped out of the motor home and smelled the waste water treatment plant. Uh oh.

Here are some things our campgrounds told us about:

They offer horseback riding on extensive trails, nightly hayrides, free Wi-Fi and a country setting.

Some things they didn't tell us:

Your campsite will be reached by going down a cliff that any sensible person wouldn't attempt on horseback, much less in a motor home. The hay wagon does not have any hay. The free Wi-Fi will wipe out your computer with absolutely no warning and when you restore it there will be no virus protection.   The country setting is bounded by a water processing plant on one side and very possibly the biggest landfill in all of Ohio, or even more possibly, the entire country, on the other.

The autumn leaves have been very pretty though...

A Train Ride, a Canal Boat and Fall Colors

To my amazement, I actually got to sleep last night with the thump, thump, thump coming from the water waste treatment facility right outside our door. It was like trying to sleep with a giant alien heartbeat pulsing through your head.

But, morning came early. We actually didn't need to get up quite so early but Joe and I had some miscommunication about what time we needed to be in Akron to catch our train. So, when the alarm went off at 7 a.m. we were in good shape to make our 11 a.m. train departure. Yawn. We did head out plenty early just to be sure we could find the station. As we pulled out I was amazed to see campers already out around their fire pits and enjoying the out of doors. Apparently if you put a picnic table and a campfire in the shadow of Mount Garbage, no one cares that there is a giant landfill within sniffing distance. I don't know, but I sure wouldn't drink the water here.

We had a beautiful day with steadily clearing skies and fall colors in all their glory. Proves once again, no amount of planning replaces dumb luck. I really had no assurance that the leaves would even be on the trees yet by now or that the sun would shine. We really couldn't have had a much nicer day to enjoy our trip by vintage train car through the Cuyahoga National Park. The three hour round trip included a chance to stretch at the Visitor's Center. We got an educational presentation on the role of the canal system in settling the Ohio wilderness. Why wasn't history this interesting when I was in school?

On our return trip the train was more crowded and we ended up sitting with a pleasant lady who needed extra room since she just had knee surgery. Her brother and his new girlfriend were in the seat ahead of us. I'd guess the dating couple was mid-60s in age. I didn't get a look at him but I'd say unless the guy was a real troll he probably could have done better than his current companion. But, as they say, there's someone for everyone. Maybe she has a nice personality. I shudder to think of ever getting back in the dating game at this age. I'd be the one with the nice personality (at least until he got to know me better).

I'd love to include a few pictures of our train trip, but Joe left his brand new high tech, high end Canon camera I got him for his birthday, back at the RV. I, of course had my camera. Only problem is, I left the SD card in my computer (back in the RV) and the batteries were croaked. Oh well.

We headed back to camp by following the "Ohio and Erie Canalway America's Byway". On our route was the little town of Canal Fulton. We stopped but unfortunately we missed the last running of the canal boat for the year which was the previous weekend. But it was still enjoyable to walk around the little town. Just like Akron and much of this part of Ohio, Canal Fulton has all kinds of opportunities for trail walking, riding and outdoor recreation. Another surprise – but that's what travel is all about!

Chapter 12

Good Driving Joe! October 23, 2012

Wow-we went uppity up-up we went down da down down…the hills of Pennsylvania are a lot more like mountains but the Flamingo flew steadily and hopefully we'll do ok in the 'real' mountains. We headed east and north through the Clarion river valley and surprise! The fall color was still amazing even in the north.

What we didn't know until we got here was that they usually have snow by now. Yikes. But we have lucked out with a week of Indian summer; temps in the 60's and yesterday we even hit 70 degrees. After consulting two maps and two GPS systems, we found our destination outside of Leeper, PA.

I had recently contacted my childhood friend, Sandy by searching on the internet. We moved to Bridge Street when I was four and Sandy's house was directly across the street. She was two years ahead of me in school but only about a year and a half older than me. As little children we played after school several days a week and as teenagers we rode our bikes, played tennis and badminton, and just hung out. When I was 'homeless' after Joe was drafted and I couldn't afford my apartment, Sandy and her husband took me in for a few weeks as I bounced from my parents to my aunt and uncle's to whomever else would put up with me. Sandy and her husband Dean lived in Ohio and after several years we just somehow lost track of one another. They moved again, we moved, they moved…long story short, somehow thirty five years had gone by and we hadn't seen or heard from them.

The big bus pulled up in front of Cook Forest Emporium, Sandy and Dean's retirement dream come true, an eclectic antique and vintage wares store housed in a rustic barn and an old farm house in the heart of a popular tourist area. They generously welcomed us into their home at the back of the property and poured wine, fed us dinner and basically answered the question, "So what have you been doing for the last thirty plus years?"

I couldn't help but think of how amazing it is to live in these times. A hundred fifty years ago if your friend moved away you might not even know if they lived to make the journey. Mail service was not always reliable; there was no telephone – much less an internet to search. When I found Sandy and called her it was just coincidence that her parents were visiting at that time. And last night, Sandy told me they had just been talking about my family right before I called. I am continually amazed at how things are just out there in the universe. If that makes no sense to you, never mind. And if it does, I don't need to explain, do I?

Pennsylvania - Hills, Hershey's and Hurricane

We enjoyed some really great time with our friends who fed us and acted as tour guides for our stay. A highlight was spending a day at the sight of the first oil well find in America. It was interesting, educational and included a terrific meal at Oil Can Johnny's – a great home-style restaurant our friends enjoy.

Before we knew it, Wednesday morning came and we had reservations for a rustic campground on the curiously named "Pinch Road" in central Pennsylvania. If I thought we were on Mr. Toad's wild ride before, oh boy. I felt a little green by the time we got to our camp. I was starting to get a headache too, but that could have been because the campground was right next to a shooting range. The booming report of gunfire was nonstop. I guess we were lucky to be here in the fall because the staff assured us that the shooters knock off at dark and it gets dark about 6:30 – thankfully. After getting set up we realized that the highway we had passed over seemingly several miles away was actually next to the campground. By the time we twisted and turned, we ended up right next to the major four lane. Unbelievable. No kidding, they do not put this stuff on their websites and brochures.

We have had a really good time since being here however. Yesterday we toured Longwood Gardens which were amazingly beautiful even at this time of the year. The gardens surround the summer retreat of the legendary tycoon Pierre DuPont –well, let's just say that it just proves again-if you have enough vision, money and labor you can do anything. We ate waaaay too much Pennsylvania Dutch good cooking for dinner. Darn it's not my fault – the pie was included in the meal!

Today we enjoyed a surprise at the little town of Lititz, PA. We went there in search of the Wilbur Candy factory and found the first pretzel factory in the USA and a charming town full of history, too.

From there it was Hershey, PA and a fun tour of Hershey World. There is one thing we've found, when you visit someplace, be it cookies, candy, blown glass, whatever – there are no bargains just because you're at the "world headquarters". I can get a better buy on Hershey's chocolates at Meijer's just about any time. And yet there were tons of chocolates, stuffed animals and other souvenirs being toted away. Go figure.

A Flamingo and an Armadillo Go to Washington

Well, the on-going weather crisis changed our plans this morning once and for all. It looked like Hurricane Sandy was going to hit Pennsylvania for sure and we decided it would be a good idea to be someplace else by then. Our son's in-laws had lined up entertainment for our visit that we'd have to miss. We were glad to find out that the tickets we couldn't use were going to go to our daughter-in-law's sister and family. We talked to our son's mother and father-in-law, Mae and Sandy one more time, then called ahead to our next stop in Fredericksburg, Virginia and found that we could get in a day early, so we packed up and headed off for the approximately three hour drive south.

Remember how Gilligan and the passengers set sail for a 'three hour cruise'??? That is how our day went. First of all, Joe decided he didn't want to take the toll road. I don't know how much the toll would have been but I can tell you that in retrospect, no price would have been too much to pay. We set off once again, up and down, up and down, over, around and through the Pennsylvania countryside. Now, if I didn't mention it before, there are two outstanding things about Pennsylvania driving – no, make that three. Most of the roads are impossibly narrow. Almost every turn is a 90 degree angle. Finally, Pennsylvania drivers are totally nuts. I was less than thrilled at the thought of a longer drive than absolutely necessary but it was not all that far to the interstate so I figured what the heck. Mistake number one.....

Finally, we got to I-83 and I figured ok, now we're on the way. I talked to my sister- in- law after eleven a.m. and it was already over an hour into our three hour drive but at least we were finally on a highway without hairpin turns, one lane bridges and houses that were built right up to the curb. Whew. That was until everything came to a complete and total stop with a major traffic jam. After sitting for about half an hour, Joe decided to pull off an incredible completely lateral move to get us on the exit ramp and off the highway. OK. We set the GPS to route us off the highway and after looking at the turn by turn it appeared that there would be a few turns to make but we would end up back on I-95 headed for Virginia – no problem. Another mistake...

Well, we made turns all right. One after another after another... Soon it was after 1 p.m. and it was clear we had no earthly idea where we were. Now, here's something you might not have considered: it is hard to figure out a new route when you don't know where you are to begin with! Of course, the fact that we missed at least two of our turns which made the poor GPS lady have to say, "Recalculating, recalculating." didn't help. The roads became more and more congested, narrower and with a stop light every few yards. That's when I saw a sign that said "Chevy Chase Library". Uh, oh. I remembered being in Chevy Chase a number of years ago and it was right outside of Washington DC. As the Flamingo Express lumbered through tiny streets clogged with traffic and pedestrians, I noticed a couple taking pictures of us as we passed by. Somehow I'm pretty sure that a 33' motor home pulling a full size Jeep is not a common sight.

We finally pulled onto a hinky little weird side street that paralleled the main street, trying to get our bearings. That's when we hit the tree. Well, not exactly. We hit the tree limbs as we pulled *away* from the curb, having determined that we were hopelessly lost. We sheared off part of the doodad that holds the awning and put a pretty good long 'scuff' in the awning itself – but we missed hitting any other cars or houses.

There was hardly enough room for a small car much less a full size motor home. At one point I was crying quietly but fortunately Joe didn't hear me (I said it was quietly). I was amazed that Joe was able to maneuver us out of the twisting little streets with cars parked on both sides. This was just after we passed the National Cathedral. I couldn't believe we were in Washington D.C.! First of all, we hadn't planned to visit D.C. at all! Secondly, we were lost. And thirdly, well – I don't know what was thirdly. By the time we whizzed by the Washington Monument I was pretty much laughing hysterically.

Just after crossing the George Washington Bridge, we saw the highway to get to I-95. Thank God! It was now after 4 p.m. and we were still over an hour and a half from our campsite. Keep in mind; we had left Pennsylvania at 10:15 a.m. for a three hour drive. At this point I had come to two conclusions: 1.) I want to go home and 2.) Motor home travel is not my cup of tea.

The trip from Washington to Fredericksburg was truly lovely with the sun finally making an appearance after four days. The turning leaves were a nice distraction from the eight lanes of traffic all roaring along at ten to thirty miles over the limit. We were passed on the left, the right, cut off, squeezed into our lane and almost clipped by a moron on her phone. Other than that it was quite pleasant.

Finally we turned onto a curving country lane and pulled into our campground. A kids' Halloween trick or treat was in full swing so we had to make our way carefully to our hook up so that we didn't squash any little ghosties or goblins that were running around with total abandon. I was so happy to stop moving! I was beyond being upset or even nervous. Somewhere around the border of Virginia I had totally lost all ability to relate to reality. So, when Joe went to hook up to utilities and discovered we had left our water filter and hookup regulator behind back in Pennsylvania I wasn't even surprised.

So, as long as we had to go buy a new filter/regulator, we decided to go out for Chinese food. I've got to tell you, it is very, very difficult to stay motivated to follow a good diet plan when you can't be sure if any given meal might be your last…

Hunkered Down in Virginia

UPDATE:

We are safe and sound (so far) in the wild woods of Virginia. Of course about five miles away is every fast food, convenience and shopping venue you can imagine, all housed in one strip mall after the other, but right here feels like the middle of nowhere.

We've decided to stay put until the hurricane weather decides what exactly it is going to do. This area is braced for power outages but at least we won't be on the roads in high winds. The only concern is that this park was flooded with the last really bad tropical storm and one of their buildings floated away.....

But Joe is convinced this is the better place to be. We'll call tomorrow and see what is predicted in Williamsburg, which is right on the Atlantic. At least this gave me a chance to do laundry and clean up the coach a little bit – and take a nap! So, it might not be so bad waiting out the storm here. The woods are really lovely and with a little imagination you can hear the rustle of boots through the leaves and the report of guns as the confederate and union soldiers took up their positions. This area is full of battlefields, historic markers and sites of historical significance. If the weather ever clears up maybe we'll even see some of them.....

From One Disaster to Another-

Well, we were wise to get the heck out of Pennsylvania but in retrospect we should probably have kept on going. Of course, the three hour drive to Fredericksburg that ended up being more like eight hours was a factor. By the time we got here, hurricane Sandy was bearing down on the eastern seaboard; we figured we were best to hunker down here and stay put until the storm passes.

Today we woke up to find that Virginia has also been declared a disaster area. Seems that the path of the storm turned inland sooner than expected which means we are now pretty much in the eye of the storm. Oops. Well, we're here now...you may recall that God told Noah to build the ark BEFORE it started raining. Bottom line - it's a little late to hit the road now. We are located between a pond on one side and a creek on the other. Joe, being the eternal optimist that he is, has pronounced the pond is half empty; I see it as half full. If the Flamingo Express has to learn to float I guess we'll find out who is right.

Needless to say, we had some discussion about whether to go to stay at this campground and whether or not to move to higher ground if we did stay here. Short story: we're still here and we're still in the same spot. I know it seems like I'm the bossy one, but you'd be amazed how often Joe gets his way. On the other hand, he just left to go get me ice cream. I can be bribed. Yes, he's going to get soaked and it is truly miserable out but he's probably happy to go out in the storm vs. stay here with me whining.

We both took a shower and I fixed a hot breakfast while there was still power. The campground owners told us to expect power to go out anytime now. Our disaster plan is pretty simple. We bought a case of bottle water while there still was some to be found – that was good. We have bread, peanut butter and chocolate. Oh, and Excedrin. With the pressure change, naturally I got a migraine. We plan to run the generator just enough to keep the coach bearably warm and we do have our winter coats and gloves if necessary. It's raining so hard that I can't see a thing out of the windows. But, at this point, I figure every hour we are warm, dry and have electricity is an hour to the good. And to think, at home we have a generator so we never have to worry about storms. Tell me again why this travel thing is a good idea???

Chapter 13

A Good Decision October 30, 2012

Well, not much humor to be had in the aftermath of Hurricane Sandy. We were so fortunate to decide to get to this stop and then stay. Amazingly, we never lost power and didn't need to go to our emergency backup plan. The little lake/pond here at the KOA rose fast but never overflowed. We're thinking that since the last flooding here some work had been done to direct water away. Can I tell you how incredibly lucky we feel?

Watching the devastation on television we realize how close we could have been to real trouble. The Flamingo Express does not want to learn to swim. We feel so very blessed to have been safely out of the direct hit of the storm.

So, our one night in Fredericksburg, VA has turned out to be four and we haven't even seen as much as a historical marker as far as sightseeing, but that's ok. We've stayed in, read, relaxed, napped and snacked.

We're off to historic Williamsburg tomorrow and the forecast is for a nice day. So, we're back about our business of shoring up the economy, spending our children's inheritance as we go. Whatever we can do to help!

So, you know, it just occurred to me today that since we retired last year that we've both packed on some pounds and at the same time, while we've been traveling the food we've gotten has been less than fantastic. Come to think of it, most of the better meals we've had are ones we've fixed here in the RV. And those have been pretty simple and far from gourmet. Most of travel involves enjoying local cuisine, trying delicious new things and indulging in a few special treats. Somehow, we have not always picked the winners.

After touring the Williamsburg Museum, we asked the nice lady at the information desk where was a good place to eat? She suggested a seafood place. And wow, it did sound great. That was until we looked at the menu posted outside. Entrées started at $22.00 and everything was a la carte. Yikes. We just wanted dinner, not to invest in their business! She also recommended a backup choice where the hamburgers were 'the best in town'. They also had to be the most expensive. There were exactly two burgers to choose from, one at $12.99 and another at $11.99. But they DID come with fries. We thought about seeing if we could split one but then I remembered I'd seen a place with pizza and subs. By now I was soooo hungry, pizza sounded really great and I figured it couldn't be as expensive as a $30.00 piece of fish. It was pretty much a no frills place and we stepped up to the counter to order. After ordering, the young man at the register let us know we would have to take our pizza to go because they were closing. Joe told him we didn't have any place to go to eat it. I asked what time they closed?? It was only 7 p.m. It seems that closing time was a rather fluid concept.

So, there we stood going back and forth-would they stay open long enough for us to eat, should we cancel our order, could we maybe eat the pizza in the shuttle bus? We were the first customers they'd had all day and they had just decided to close up but they would make our pizza and stay open until we ate it. To their utter dismay, some other poor schmuck came in and wanted to order while we were still there. By that time they had shut down the soda machines so he couldn't get a soft drink with his order. I wasn't sure they were going to even give him a glass of water.

Well, we sat down and very quickly-our pizza arrived. Somehow our $12.99 pizza cost over $15.00 but it smelled delicious and the sauce was really tasty. I was so hungry that I got about halfway through the first piece before I realized the crust was very, very doughy. Joe asked if I wanted to send it back. Ha ha ha ha ha. Like I'm giving these guys who really want to close up and probably get to a Halloween party, a chance to spit on my pizza. Uh, NO. I scraped up the topping and nibbled on the crust and then just gave it up. At least we didn't order the large!

But here's the thing: I know there are great restaurants everywhere but for some reason, we just haven't found many of them on this trip so far. I guess we'll be doing more eating 'in' unless we hear of something really outstanding or develop a taste for overpriced burgers and undercooked pizza. Right now I'd settle for some leftover Halloween candy.

Colonial Williamsburg, Virginia

Last night we went to the Colonial Williamsburg Visitor Center just to get an idea of what exactly it is here. I'd read the information and brochures and still hadn't figured out just how this works. I sort of pictured a theme park/city and it kind of is…but I couldn't imagine if there was like an entrance gate to the whole city or what? You have to get tickets, so???

At the Visitor's Center we got the scoop. The Historic part of the city is open to the public but you have to have a paid admission to get into any of the homes, museums and historic venues. No wonder I was confused. It's really a city but at the same time it's an attraction. People actually live in the private homes among the displays and colonial workshops.

We paid up, got photographed and badged and with a "one day only" special we got admission to the end of the year. What a deal! Obviously we won't be here for two more months, but this way we can go back for as many days as we want while we're here for the same price as one day.

. And now we know what Colonial Williamsburg is all about!

Sometimes I'm Such an Idiot

Today we decided we'd had a couple days of Colonial America in a row, so we'd go for some of today's USA with a trip to Norfolk, VA where the U.S. Navy fleet is based.

We got off to a kind of late start but the weather looked promising to be outdoors so we decided the forty-five minute trip would be an easy drive. We found the right place after trying to enter the restricted naval base where we <u>thought</u> the tour was. Oops. In the Navy tour office a very nice young ensign gave us a heads up that if we took the military tour we wouldn't be able to take pictures but if we drove into Norfolk to the museum and boat tour we could, on a civilian cruise, take all the pics we wanted. We decided to drive on into town and with the help of GPS we found the Museum complex and were immediately baffled by the fact that there was absolutely no parking. After circling the lot a couple of times, Joe decided to let me off to check it out. Of course I went to the wrong window first, but I finally found the boat tour and got the scoop. Next tour at 2 p.m. – deal! That gave us time enough for a quick lunch, get back, and figure out a place to park and get the tickets.

What we didn't take into account was that there was absolutely, positively no parking available anywhere near downtown. We found plenty of restaurants but no parking spots. Finally we decided it would be quicker to drive out of town where we could park and then come back rather than continue to fight the traffic. I asked our GPS lady to take us to a DQ, figuring that would be farther out. Surprise! There was one just a few blocks away – and miraculously, it had a small parking lot behind. We parked, piled out, walked around the corner and discovered that the Dairy Queen had gone out of business. Arghhhh! We decided to try the sub shop next door. Luckily, it was good and pretty well priced. I couldn't understand the guy at the counter so we accidently ended up without cheese and with onions…not exactly what we had in mind but it was good, quick and close enough to make the tour.

It was getting late so Joe dropped me off and went to put the car in a parking garage we had located. He came jogging up the street about the time I had given him up for lost. 4th floor – that was the first thing he told me. Don't forget the car is on the 4th floor. OK.

Well, I had gotten the tickets while waiting for Joe and I repeated to him what the ticket sales girl had said – go to the next building with the three windows. Ok. We hustled over to the building and something didn't look right. There was no one around at all. We decided to take the elevator up to the main area and see if that was the right place.

So, two things: If I had looked at the tickets which clearly showed the name of the boat and then looked at the boat tied up next to the building I would have probably figured out we were just supposed to walk over there and board. Or, knowing that people give lousy directions, I should have asked more questions. Oh, well.

Luckily we found a lady who pointed out the waiting boat so we hustled back down the steps, across the park and made it before they cast off. It started off as a nice smooth ride but as the day went on it got rougher and rougher. Everyone was asked to come inside and to remain seated. If you know my sailing ability, you might think I got seasick but nope, I kept it together. The only thing that made me queasy was the price tag on our naval war ships. The nuclear powered ships that are crewed by 6000 sailors have a price tag of eight billion each-yupper do-that's Billion with a B…eight billion smackeroos. If that doesn't make your head spin I don't know what will. No wonder the federal government is hurting. Can you imagine? Feeding the crew would be like making meals for all of my home town, Otsego and half of neighboring Plainwell. And that's on top of the initial price tag for the big boat itself. PLUS probably a few extras like equipment, pay, medical benefits – those incidentals.

We got back safely although a little too late to take a tour of the museum. We set out for the parking garage and quickly made our way up to the 4th floor. Joe was sure where he had left the Jeep but nope-it wasn't there. We looked around the entire floor. No car. We tracked back to the elevator – yup, we were on the right floor. Finally we decided we would just have to trot around the floors below until we found it. Turned out this was one weird numbering system. There were sort of 'split level' areas between floors – logically our car would have been on maybe, 3 ½…..but at least we found it. Another exciting day and safely back to our home away from home. Whew.

Walk on the Wild Side

Today was one of those serendipitous happenings kinds of days. Joe decided to go to for a ride in the opposite direction of our campground here near Williamsburg. Our tentative plan for the day was to go do some shopping but I guess I was puddling around in the shower too long or sorting laundry...don't know why he went, but I'm so glad he did. He discovered a gem of a Virginia State Park that overlooks the York River. The views were so amazing – I think we could see all the way out to the Chesapeake Bay.

He came back to get me and we set off to do a little hiking. Now, we'd had a couple of days doing the "colonial" thing, a day touring the Naval Station and Norfolk and we'd done the museums and tour of historic homes. It was definitely time for a little outdoors.

We started at the ranger station which was pretty much deserted but had a good map of the trails available; that's all we really needed. We started on the three mile loop, which sounded pretty easy. "Moderate difficulty and only three miles"- piece of cake. I reminded myself after the first long hill that I often walk farther than that in a shopping mall or at the outlet stores. Of course, the malls don't have hills. Or tree roots, low hanging branches, muck, uneven boards on bridges with no handrails.....ah, but I digress. Seriously, it was picture perfect really, all kidding aside. The sky was a cloudless brilliant blue, the forest was quiet and peaceful, and we enjoyed the cool air, warm sun, the smell of pine and the beauty of the changing leaves.

Joe actually took a picture of "fat girl hiking" (me). I may not be a little woodland sprite or scamper up the grades and down the ravines like a graceful doe but we did have a great time. We caught our breath after the first hike and did another hike around the fresh water lake and woods trails. It was a beautiful, perfect day.

A beautiful place to take a hike

The Historic "Triangle"

Boy, it is nice to be seeing this great county and not standing in line to vote. When you are here in the area that was the nursery to our infant democracy, it becomes more real than any history lecture could ever make it. The hardships and sacrifices made for the past 230+ years so that I could cast a vote feel very real to me today. And I'm glad we got our ballots in before we hit the road.

If you come to the Williamsburg area, be sure you don't miss the nearby Jamestown and Yorktown venues. Taken together, the three bring you through the first early struggles to establish a settlement in what would become Virginia, the War for Independence and the establishment of the fledgling United States of America. We have seen so much, learned so much, that it would take pages and pages to give you every detail but let me hit some highlights.

At Williamsburg, pony up for the tickets that get you into all the various demonstrations etc. You can certainly enjoy the experience by only participating in the presentations that are open to everyone but you will MISS SO MUCH! I initially thought it was kind of pricey but when you understand everything involved - not really. Shuttle buses run all day every day. The central wardrobe has more than 1800 outfits for the presenters to help bring the life and times of the early patriots to life for you. There are animals, equipment, buildings, presentations and people that support the experience. It is unlike anything I've ever seen. You will step back in time to the day to day struggles of 1774-1776.

Or if you want to keep more of a time line intact, start with Jamestown. I recommend the National Park. First of all, Joe has the senior America pass, so we got in for absolutely $0. The main display building offers a fantastic big screen movie and an accompanying exhibit that do a great job of explaining what the first settlers to Virginia had to deal with. Then on to the archeological exhibits; see how the past comes to life through today's science. And finally, the museum on the grounds is worth your time: well done and well thought out exhibits. We were fortunate enough to be visiting during the unique presentation by a Native American dressed in a magnificent coyote skin cape and traditional garb as he explained how the inhabitants of the new world would have been living in the 1700s. He brought history to life in a unique way that I will always remember. He was a very traditional individual with a keen sense of who he was and where he came from…he also had his website address on the side of his trailer.

A Pig in a Poke

We've really enjoyed our time immersing ourselves in the history of colonial times here in the Williamsburg area. But, you can only learn so much and then it's time for…Shopping!

Yesterday I laid out my shopping campaign for today. Those Revolutionaries weren't the only ones who could draw up a battle plan! High on my list was to search out some Virginia peanuts and some Smithfield ham. I didn't really know if I could even properly prepare a Smithfield ham and I had a top price limit in mind, so those were two limiting factors. We set out in search of answers.

First of all we did a little outlet shopping – hey, they were here, how could I not go?? Then we headed for the ferry that crosses the James River so we could get to Smithfield, home to the famous hams. I had the address for the Visitor Center but that was about all. Still, we found our way in good shape although I have to say we didn't see a single pig. Turned out the only pigs we saw all day were the painted ones around downtown that the various businesses sponsored – and they were concrete.

The Visitor Center gave us a detailed map for a walking tour of the historic home district that featured many wonderful examples of Victorian architecture as well as homes dating back to the 1700s. We also got a short history lesson on the Smithfield Ham. Like Champagne that is so called because it can only come from the Champagne region of France, only a Smithfield produced ham can be called a genuine Smithfield.

Before leaving Williamsburg, we had a great lunch at a plantation-Old Chickahominy House, where we were served thin slivers of very salty ham on a thin, tender biscuit. Quite delicious (but salty). Well, Smithfield ham is salty because the process involves soaking the meat in salt for a long, long time. Then it is slow smoked using a process that varies depending on the smokehouse operator's recipe. The bottom line is that the final product is a salty, mummified looking thing that can last for months. Or years, as it turns out. In the town's museum we saw the world's oldest ham. No kidding. It is like 100 years old and supposedly is still edible. Quite a shelf life...yuck.

You'd think that would discourage me but I still had to shop for ham. I don't know exactly how this stuff is priced but a very small ham was $79.95. We couldn't find anything that showed how many pounds it was. Joe summed it up: too salty, too expensive and too much trouble. Ok, skip the ham; how about peanuts? These people are nuts (no pun intended). Basically it seems if you put peanuts in the shell into a burlap sack, put a cutesy label on showing that they are 'Virginia Peanuts', you can sell them for $13.95 for 12 ounces. I'm pretty sure these are the same peanuts you can get at the grocery store for about 3 bucks a pound.

Ok, no ham, no peanuts but a fun day in Virginia and tomorrow- on to North Carolina for one night, then Charleston, South Carolina.

Chapter 14

November 9, 2012

Lord have mercy! Praying, a lot of praying is what I did in Charleston traffic last night as we alternately zoomed or screeched to a halt in unbelievable traffic. It was just a nightmare…

Honestly, I don't know if we were in different city, or if thirty years of change have made this much difference, but Charleston is nothing, *nothing* at all as I remember it. We were here probably twenty to thirty years ago and what I remember is a slow, genteel, leisurely paced town. We took the horse and carriage ride through the city with "Billy Bob" – a character we've never forgotten. I think if he's still here he's been run down and paved over.

The traffic is six lanes everywhere, wall to wall vehicles, all of which seem to be in a lane three lanes over from where they are going next. We did get to the old part of town but that was absolutely worse. After 45 minutes of trying endlessly to find a parking space, including sitting for ten minutes in a 'Public Parking' lot trying to find someone to pay or tell us if we would get towed (no one ever did appear), we gave it up. We were going to sample one of Charleston's great restaurants but unless you're lucky enough to find a place to park – forget it!

Charleston is rated as one of the top 100 tourist destinations. I can see why. I think all of the tourists are here right now and they're all in my traffic lane. Good grief. I am so glad we didn't end up here for four days –we can't get out of here soon enough. Even our park is a little worrisome. Any of you who have known us since we went to Alaska, know that I have a rule about anywhere I visit: I want to be at the top of the food chain. On the information for our park here, it warns that there are "wild alligators" in our pond….what? You were expecting <u>tame</u> alligators?? Actually, I wasn't expecting any alligators…enough said. On to Savannah - let's hope there's some southern charm and no southern crazy.

Doing the Charleston November 9, 2012 – continued

Well, here was our one full day in Charleston: After fighting the insane traffic last night the idea of going back to the city was like, 'seen it, done it, over it'. We decided to do some laundry and go to the store.

At the laundry facility I was talking to a nice gal who has been a 'full timer' with the husband for eleven years. She said her kids keep asking when they are going to settle down and stay put but when she asks them who is going to pour a pad in the backyard that shuts them up again for another year. She said they have left their car at the Visitor Center in Charleston then taken the free trolley to visit the city. So, if you ever want to go, try that.

We've met such nice people RVing. After talking to my laundry day partner I thought once again how people seem to just get along so well on the road. Then it occurred to me that you never get to know people well enough to find out if they are real jerks. Maybe that's it.

We finished our laundry and errands before 2 o'clock. With the whole afternoon left we decided to check out the greater Charleston area. So, we did.

I'm usually able to brag that when we're thrown out of someplace that we've been 'thrown out of better places than *this*.' Today set a whole new standard for the better places. We have NEVER been thrown out of a high rent district like this one. We headed on to the island of Kiawah which is adjacent to Charleston. First of all, we didn't realize the entire island is like one huge gated community. Well, we talked our way through the guard house entrance, looking for the "visitor center", which I helpfully pointed to on my map. The guard looked puzzled but nicely directed us to try the "Sanctuary" for information about the island. Sanctuary turned out to be a hotel complex with a parking lot chock full of Beemers, Lexus, Jaguar and other high end vehicles – and one Jeep (us). We walked up to the place like we could actually afford to stay there….I have never so totally felt like I was at the lower end of the socio-economic scale. This place appears to be home to – not the top 10%; more like the top ½ of 1%. .

I will say the lady we talked to in one of the shops at the hotel was very polite. I'm sure she didn't notice I was wearing my baggy four year old Walmart clearance shirt and Joe had on 'no name' jeans. I'm surprised she didn't recommend one of their $200.00 scarves to compliment my outfit. Yeah, right.

By then our cover story was that we were looking for the county park and she very kindly directed us. So, we were back in the Jeep; blew past the guard and left the lifestyles of the rich and richer behind us.

Turned out the ocean was just as blue when seen from the county park, the waves just as mesmerizing, the sun as warm and the sky as brilliant as the best summer's day ever. You're only as poor as you let yourself feel…

November 10, 2012

We got out of Charleston - barely. The gas station situation was going to be a problem for filling up before leaving so we ended up with me driving the Jeep separately so Joe could pull the motor home up to the pump and then make the turn out. Of course the station was just packed and as I pulled in there were 3 more cars behind me, making it impossible for me to just have a sec to figure out where to park. The guy behind me blasted his horn – thank you, Southern hospitality. I parked, trotted over to the RV and asked Joe where I should pull up to hitch up after fueling. At the same time, an elderly (again, translate "anyone older than me") gentleman was also talking to me. He seemed to be getting quite a kick out of our situation. Between the second conversation and Joe's explanation we ended up in a shouting match in which Joe was rather clear that if someone is pointing you should ignore what is being said and just LOOK! Okay.

We got hooked up and on the road to Savannah which I must say was a nice drive. And along the way we spotted a billboard for "Peach cider, fresh pie and boiled peanuts". We weren't sure about two out of those three but we were pretty sure about pie. Joe said – let's stop, so we did. It was a hair raising, death defying feat to get the motor home pulled off the side of the road far enough to avoid disaster but, to the awe and astonishment of onlookers the Flamingo had landed. We put out the steps; I hopped out and made a record time pie run, only stopping to try a "boiled peanut". I must tell you, it is not something I would go out of the way to get. If you don't know, the peanut is left in the shell, boiled in water and then just kept in the water until you scoop it out and eat it. Unknowing, I almost ate the shell and all but luckily I asked first. Ok, you *shell* the peanut. The resulting treat is sort of squishy and tastes mostly like a cooked bean, only without the flavor. Uck. But the pie was good!

November 14, 2012

Hard to believe that tomorrow will be our last day on this trip. We leave the motor home here in storage on Friday and start back to Michigan for the holidays. In a way it seems like a long time ago that we were at the fabulous glass museum in Toledo yet it seems like it has been a very short trip.

Now, I have to tell you – we did a very bad thing in Savannah. After my complaining about not eating very good meals, well, as they say down south, "Shut my mouth". We had lunch at Paula Deen's restaurant, The Lady and Sons. Oh brother. Any meal that begins with blue cheese salad dressing made with real cream and ends with Paula's 'gooey cake'…..well, it was a bad, bad thing but it tasted so, so good. I have never had such delicious fried chicken. Although, I guess everyone here must make fried chicken. We have seen numerous billboards and signs around the area posted by the city of Savannah entreating citizens to "can your grease" and not dump cooking grease down the drain. Apparently that is a big problem here. Euewwwwww. Who would do that??

Our fantastic lunch wasn't the only highlight here. Savannah is an almost mystical, magical city with the massive live oaks dripping their ethereal bouquets of Spanish moss; the glow of gas lights, cobblestone streets, old mansions and antique shops, art galleries and cafes. Savannah is a great walking city. We planned to take a guided tour (either by horse and carriage or tour bus), but it is really an easy city to walk in rather than drive or ride. There are something like twenty-two public "squares" or what in today's terms would be green spaces. Each of these parks has its own character and ambiance. And I'm sure each is a major pain in the patootie for people who have to live here. We've been to galleries and museums, historic house tours, shopping and walking, walking, walking.

Part of our time here has been out of the city. We spent a day on nearby Tybee Island touring the lighthouse and the fort and another day at the State Park, walking the trails. Although it turned cooler today, this has been a great time of the year to visit. The spring is supposed to be gorgeous with everything in bloom. At least at this time the numerous types of annoying and biting bugs are pretty well gone. Speaking of things in bloom, I have a nice purple bruise blooming on my forehead. The day we went out to the island it was pretty sunny so I wore a baseball cap all day. When we got back to the motor home I popped out of the car and with my hat on I didn't look UP, so I walked squarely into the side of the slide out on the motor home. Ow. Oh well, I think it will have faded away by the time we get to Michigan. Stuff happens.

Chapter 15

On the Road Again

Well, we enjoyed a wonderful Christmas with our 20 month old grandson and then hustled Santa Claus out of town like a drunk who just blew through his last dollar at a Casino. The weather looked threatening for the trip back to Georgia but we continued with packing up, putting up and eating up everything in the house. The Christmas tree came down; the holiday décor was shuffled back up to the attic. Every nook and cranny of the Jeep was packed with three months' worth of the goodies and treats we got for Christmas and, like a couple of fat Christmas geese, Joe and I expanded our seat belts a bit, buckled up and flew south.

We arrived back at Savannah after a very lucky trip. By that I mean we missed the really bad snowstorm, the sleet in the mountains was NOT freezing on to the roads and we were five car lengths behind a really, really bad two car accident about 20 minutes out of Savannah and managed not to end up having an accident ourselves. One car was already on fire just seconds after the traffic had slowed and we realized how close we had come. Joe had to lock it up but the Jeep stopped before we plowed into the vehicle ahead of us and the guy behind us managed to stop so except for the slowdown we were ok.

We got back to the RV park (and I use the word loosely) and the storage area about 2 p.m. which put us in good shape to get the Flamingo Express out of storage, reload the clothes I dragged across eight states to wash at home so I didn't have to feed the coin laundry, get in our supplies and rest up for the trip down to Florida tomorrow. Except for one thing: there was NOBODY anywhere around and our RV was secured behind a fence with a chained and padlocked gate.

I guess I should explain a little bit about the RV Park. It is a pretty loose operation compared to anyplace else we've ever stayed. We got some of the back story on the place and it made more sense. The beautiful setting is part of a very large plantation that belonged to the grandparents/great-grandparents of the present owners. By the time they got down to the fourth generation apparently the land had been divided, possibly partly sold, divided some more and the grandchildren and their children are all scrambling around like crazy trying to find a way to make a buck. One granddaughter has a landscape business on part of the land. The young man who has the RV Park seems to be a go getter kind of guy. He also has an entertainment venue attached to the RV area and is busy adding more RV sites. His cousin actually has the Storage facility; however there is no "name" on the storage area that designates it from the RV park area...It's all rather down home and inbred. But I don't really mean to be nasty: all of them seem very hard working and the boys are just drop dead handsome (which never hurt).

Towards the back of the land is a beautiful home that is used for weddings and formal parties. It overlooks a small lake and the place just drips Southern Charm. It would be a beautiful place for a gathering. Not sure which cousins, in-laws or outlaws are in charge of that. Anyway, when we came to get the RV none of them were in evidence. Luckily, I called on my cell and the RV Park Cousin was right by the front gate, like 15 seconds away, so all was well. The Flamingo Express fired right up, Joe took it off the storage lot, we hooked up, settled in, Beaufort the armadillo woke up from his long nap, and we went off in search of a few grocery items.

You'd think that having already spent time in Savannah we'd remember how to get to a grocery store, but noooooo. We set the GPS and headed for a Kroger. Unfortunately, when we arrived at our destination, the store was no longer a Kroger and the place looked pretty seedy. The surroundings didn't look real safe either so we decided to drive on. We also had decided to get the $2 Subway sandwich deal for a quick supper. OK, you know there is a Subway on every block; sometimes two? Nope, couldn't find one. After selecting several shops that were no place to be found except in GPS land, we drove several miles to a nearly abandoned shopping plaza. There was a Subway alright and we certainly didn't have to wait in line. The really sweet girl behind the counter said a big retailer had moved out in June and the other businesses were just dying. At least we got our cheap subs so we were fortified for our quest for a grocery store.

Next thing you know-we're in downtown Savannah. Which was ok; I had actually hoped we'd have time to go visit once more. I just loved Savannah. We ended up at a Kroger that was in the heart of the city and just bustling with all kinds of people: black, white, Asian, young, old, artsy, button down conservative, you name it. And it had pie!! Oh, boy – pie! We bought our items and took one more quick tour of the city…goodbye Savannah. We loved your southern charm!

Chapter 16

"Real" Florida January 1, 2013

We arrived here yesterday afternoon to warm temperatures and a sunlit sky full of promise of good days to come. We are near the town of Ormond Beach on the Atlantic between St. Augustine and Daytona Beach. This is our first try at a State Park camping experience. And when I say experience, I mean "experience". Tomoka State Park bills itself as "the real Florida". If by that you mean the Florida that no one would ever have thought was inhabitable, you're right. Unbelievably, just a couple miles from a busy city, you find yourself on hard packed sand roads winding through overhanging palm trees, aggressive, exotic looking shrubbery and an absolute jungle of undergrowth that looks like it wouldn't be in the least intimidated by a machete. Numerous signs warn about the snakes and alligators. There should also be one about teenagers.

While we were setting up I overheard a tense conversation between a neighboring camper and her teenage daughter. Apparently the girl was campaigning to go to the store and after several times of begging, her mother snapped, "NO." The teenager did the obligatory 'eye roll' and asked why, to which her mother replied, "Because we're CAMPING!" Joy. I have to admit it is otherwise pretty quiet here and not a lot of nonstop excitement unless you're into walking, hiking and canoeing. We've heard that State Parks are generally more rustic but offer roomier, more private, spaces. Well, that's the truth. If it weren't for a glimpse of a camper in the next spot you'd swear you were in the middle of nowhere. And for us, that's great.

Getting in our spot was a little more challenge than we are used to but Joe did it. Our poor motor home was wearing a crown of Spanish moss by the time we got maneuvered into the barely big enough "driveway" and we nearly wiped out a side mirror on a palm tree but we made it. Supposedly you can get a 34' unit in here but I'd like to see it. The hard packed sand made a pretty firm surface to set up on but when we put down the leveling jacks, three wheels were completely off the ground. Somehow that didn't seem like the best idea, besides which I would need a ladder to get to our bottom step to climb in. Joe pulled out and backed in again then finally gave up and manually leveled the coach which put us back on four wheels. Nothing is running downhill when you pour a glass of something, so I guess we're level enough.

Then we hooked up. It just didn't sound right when I put out the slides but it wasn't until we tried to turn on the television we realized we were running off our batteries even though we were plugged into the 50 amp service. Uh, oh. Joe tried a couple of things to turn off and on breakers, plug and unplug the coach…it was kinda' like Chevy Chase in Christmas Vacation, trying to light his Christmas display. Finally we had power (although I don't think Joe knew why, exactly). Then the power went off again. Well, finally we gave up on the 50 amp and plugged into the 30 amp which seems to be working fine. The good news is that it wasn't anything wrong on our end. We'll address the problem with park staff after the holiday.

Joe was busy with setting up when he realized there was no place to plug in the sewer connection. It seems I forgot to check on that particular amenity. Turns out it would have been a good idea to dump in Savannah before we came here but Joe didn't bother since it was just one night. Oh well. At least we're just a couple lots down from the restrooms and showers. Of course, I detest taking care of any 'personal business' or a shower in a public place. Ick. I hated it in Junior High School gym class and I don't like it any better now. So I'm going to try passing the "sniff test" for as long as possible before I brave the shower. Hopefully we can get to the end of our week here before having to haul over to the dump station. The good news is it's a good excuse to get out of doing dishes and use the disposable plates and cutlery! And eat out!

The "real" Florida

Well, I didn't sleep worth a darn last night. I couldn't get to sleep and then when I finally DID, the smoke alarm battery picked the middle of the night to die and the stupid thing started intermittently beeping. Then first thing this morning some squirrel was Salsa dancing on the roof right over our heads. Since I couldn't get back to sleep I figured we might as well get up and get going.

We'd been in the car, in a motel room or here at the park every day since last Friday and it was definitely time for – ROAD TRIP! We planned to go back north to tour the oldest town in America, St. Augustine FL. I am positive I've been there before, but much like Charleston, either my memory is faulty (ha–like that could possibly be it!) or the place is a lot more touristy and tarted up than I remember.

Anyway, we started our journey with the classics: Joe forgot to put on sunscreen; we had to go back for sunglasses, etc. Once we hit the road we bombed along 1-95 at a good clip until I got snookered in. Yes, I KNOW better, but I fell for the ol' roadside billboard unbelievable prices and we had to pull in. Of course, they didn't really have a pound of shelled pecans for $3.99 or bags of citrus fruit for a dollar. However, if you needed some wind chimes made from alligator skulls or a naked lady coffee cup, you would be in luck. As long as we were off the highway we decided to take a slightly different route and that turned out to be nice–very scenic. One place was almost like being in a tunnel where the live oak reached over the road and made a canopy. The sun was shining and it made for a nice trip.

So we spent a pleasant day in St. Augustine with history, shops, the best clam strips I've ever eaten and walking, walking, walking followed by climbing. We did the eight stories of the historic St. Augustine Lighthouse at the end of the day. About the sixth story it occurred to me that I might have been smarter to get the cardiologist's report on my treadmill test from December, uh, like BEFORE I was on the 200th step...but, lived to tell about it so guess it was ok.

There is "Camping" and there is "RV-ing"

Ok, so you've heard me say it before, the RV lifestyle is only somewhat like camping. RVing doesn't involve any sleeping on the ground, communing with wildlife in your personal space or developing a taste for food cooked exclusively over an open flame. It's more like hotel living without people changing your sheets or someone else having slept in them first.

This State Park is coming perilously close to "camping". First of all, my manicure is utterly and completely ruined. I have practically washed the skin off my hands. Using the communal bathroom is turning me into Macbeth's wife. I just can't get my hands clean enough. I shudder to think when was the last time anyone disinfected the bathroom stall door latches or the handles on the toilets. Without a sewer hookup it's easy to fill the holding tanks in no time, which brings me to having to take a shower in a public place.

Although Joe thinks it is amusing to tell people that if anything suspicious ever happens to him that they should go looking for me but I'm telling you I will NEVER commit spousicide (I made that up). There is no way I would risk having to live the rest of my life in a place where I have to shower where hundreds of other people have used the facilities. Omg…the bathhouse here has about a ¼" layer of mud on the floor within five minutes after it is mopped. Mud is tracked into the showers, up the walls and, frighteningly, on the edges of the sink. No kidding, I've seen footprints on the sink! Strands of hair are sticking to the cement block walls everywhere like old fashioned lead icicles thrown on a Christmas tree. I really, really don't want to touch ANYTHING. I need a facial, I need a pedicure, and I need a neck massage!! I can't believe we've only been here for four days!!

The day started out overcast and rainy-not a good day for outdoor activities. We've been planning to tour a home here in Ormond Beach that was the final residence of John D. Rockefeller, the industrialist/philanthropist. "The Casements", so named because of the large number of that type of window, was winter home to Rockefeller until he died there at age 97. The place then changed hands a few times and eventually abandoned. Not unlike an abused homeless person, the "personless" home was victimized, set on fire and vandalized. By the time the city of Ormond Beach decided to purchase it, the property was in ruins. Large additions that had been made to the original house were torn down but the main house was restored and refurbished to most of its original charm.

We just caught the tour as it started and enjoyed it thoroughly. The home is now used as a Civic Center and has a busy new life with cooking classes, art classes, children's programs and special events going on throughout the year. Our guide was a lovely lady named Ingrid, originally a teacher at the college level in Germany, now a very, very active retiree in Florida. We got chatting with her after the tour and she told us about another historic home we'd like to visit: Stetson House, home of the famous hat maker. She was even so kind as to give me her home phone number, so I called her tonight for further information, which she gave me. Then we went back to The Casements for a free Art Show (with food!-what all retirees like best - free with free!) at 7 p.m.

After the early afternoon tour we decided to drive along the ocean down A1A. At least, I guess we were along the ocean - you couldn't see any of it. Basically it is now just one high rise building after the next for miles and miles. Finally we came to the end of the road and Ponce de Leon inlet, where the famous lighthouse stands. Unlike yesterday, we didn't do the climb. For one thing it was still foggy and raining. And, this is the **tallest** lighthouse in Florida; I figured I didn't need to push my luck. Yesterday's climb was high enough. We took a few pictures of the lighthouse, enjoyed browsing the museum gift shop and that pretty much wrapped up the "beach" tour.

Joe was right. Although the campgrounds were practically empty when we left today, people piled in for the weekend. It was amazing how many spaces were filled. Hey, it is RAINING!! All these happy campers are sitting around their smoky campfires in the rain just having a good old time....can I mention again how glad I am my parents never made me go camping?? Thanks Mom and Dad, may you rest in peace.

Well, we are inside now for the night, warm and dry. No TV reception here but at least we have the internet and cell phones. Going with our AT&T phone as our internet 'hot spot' was the smartest thing we've done. I'm all for getting away from it all – just not quite this far! Especially since I got an email today from Consumers Energy that they have our bill messed up again. How can you suddenly not be able to do a debit from the same account you've been accessing for four years for automatic bill pay? All we'd need is for them to turn the power off at home. Guess I'll find out on Monday…..

Chapter 17

The Atlantic Tour Continues

After a nice, relaxing, uneventful week at Port St. Lucie, we packed up and headed out for our gateway to the Everglades: Florida City. We'll definitely make a side trip to the Everglades National Park but as the old saying goes, "It's a great place to visit but I don't really want to live there." Also on the agenda: the Keys.

But first, the journey. Our friends the Bolyens advised that we take the toll road and avoid going on the highway through Miami. Joe looked up the cost, and although I thought we should just buy a 'Sun Pass' and use the toll roads, he decided that $16.50 was just too expensive to go toll road. Well, we started out ok, pretty much. Like most roads here, we couldn't turn across traffic from the RV Park driveway which meant the GPS wanted us to do a U-turn. Luckily, Joe thought better of that idea and with only a short drive out of the way we got headed south and the GPS lady got her bearings, the Jeep was dutifully trailing along behind us and we were on our way

The closer we got to Miami the worse the traffic got. And, I kept hearing the theme song from *CSI, Miami* in my head-it was driving me nuts. I'll tell you one reason I believe our friends recommended the toll road. There was absolutely, positively not one single place to pull over the entire way, much less a "rest stop" on the highway we took. It was just traffic, traffic, traffic, insane six lanes, sometimes bumper to bumper, traffic. I saw some people do things that were just beyond the label "stupid". We really need something more descriptive than the word stupid. It might have been because the heavy traffic was confusing, but when we needed to get over onto the Palmetto Expressway, I pointed out to Joe that the signs indicated that we needed to get off onto the right hand lanes to catch it. But, the GPS lady kept insisting that we stay in the left lane. Guess who has the credibility when it comes to directions? *So* not me...but it looked to me that since we hadn't gotten over and THEN stayed in the left lane that we were going to be on the wrong highway.

Eventually it became clear that was the case when we had no choice but to go on the toll road. Now, let me say a word about the toll road. It is about as confusing as anything I've ever seen. Apparently there are places that unless you already purchased a pass there is no way to pay the toll, which results in a fairly hefty fine. And according to the lady at the desk here in the park where we are staying, the state of Florida WILL find you. Then when there **is** a place to pay, as you enter it is SO confusing that you end up either cutting someone off or being cut off trying to get into the lane to pay. We managed to get into the cash lane and Joe was going to get his money's worth out of having to pay the toll, so he held up traffic while he asked the attendant how to get to the road we needed. She was very nice, but unfortunately she didn't give the directions in English. At least not English either one of us understood. So we went hopefully on after paying our $3.00 and decided to take the first turn which then took us into a very heavy traffic area of shopping malls. Joe bravely pulled into the first parking lot so we could look at the map, try reprogramming the GPS and hopefully find our way. As long as we were parked (remember I said there were NO rest stops) I decided to take advantage of having our own bathroom on board.

All of a sudden I felt the motor home jerk! My Lord, I didn't know if someone ran into us, or if Joe suddenly took off or what. Good thing I had already peed or I would have definitely wet my pants. I yelled, "Are we moving? Are we moving?" I mean, I couldn't believe Joe would just take off while I was "indisposed"! Turned out he thought another car was going to block us in where we were parked (it didn't) and he decided to get back out to the street. I can't imagine what the look was on my face. So, we got back out in traffic and somehow turned back onto the toll road. Within a block we came to the toll booth and had to pay another $3.00. Somehow it cost us $6.00 to go approximate four blocks.

We finally saw the road we needed to be on and Joe made a dynamic move with a four lane switch. I don't think he saw the poor sap he almost sideswiped. The guy turned around in his seat, looked back at us and even from three car lengths away I could see all the blood had drained out of his face. I know my depth perception is not good but we missed swerving into this guy by millimeters, seriously. I had already spent a good part of the day alternately holding onto the armrests with a death grip and trying to brake by pressing my foot into the carpet. After that I just shut my eyes. Joe couldn't tell anyway, I had on my sunglasses and presumably he was looking at the road.

We finally rolled into Southern Comfort RV Resort in Florida City, Florida and you know what? We have a bottle of Southern Comfort on board and for those of you who know I enjoy a Southern Comfort Manhattan from time to time; you can darn well bet I had myself a double. Whew!

A Surprise-the Good Kind

Yesterday we decided to drive into the Everglades National Park. Wow. It was totally NOT what I had expected. The Welcome Center outside the park itself is a beautiful facility with information desk, knowledgeable people and resources to help you get the most from your visit. There are exhibits, trail maps, brochures and a nice gift shop. That's before you even get into the park. Our first "wild animal" sighting was right at the entrance where a poisonous cottonmouth snake was hanging out in the waterway below the bridge. He looked about as menacing as an old bicycle tire. Of course, that was probably because I was about 30 feet above him.

I mentioned before that Joe has the National Park pass so entrance fees are the biggest bargain ever. It does crack me up though…every time you use the pass the park employee will ask you, "Whose pass is this?" Are there people really stupid enough to go, "Oh, well this is my brother–in-law Jake's and I'm just borrowing it." I mean, who do you think people are going to say it belongs to??? So, anyway-we went through that charade and drove into the park.

The first stop in the park started with an ominous warning. Several signs informed you that vultures could cause damage to your vehicle. Several people had come equipped with tarps and tie downs to protect their cars. We asked one couple who was covering their vehicle and they told us vultures will tear out the black rubbery stuff around windows or sometimes just peck at the body so hard that it damages that paint. Not sure our auto insurance covers that! But we left the Jeep to fend for himself and went past the Visitor's Center and lovely picnic area to the Anhinga Walk. The Anhinga is an amazing diving bird that lives on fish although its wings are not oily like most water birds. If it doesn't dry itself out it will get waterlogged and drown. They are very large and look quite regal as they spread their wings to dry.

The walk takes you out to their nesting area through several changes of habitat. The trail is a combination of boardwalks and concrete pathways that are well marked with informational placards and great viewing of tons of wildlife. We saw practically every bird that lives in Florida and it seemed like every alligator, too. Believe me, there is no need to pay to go to an Alligator Farm, those things were everywhere! Hard to believe they were ever on the brink of extinction. The trail is just incredibly well done and made so that it is easily accessible, even in a wheelchair or with a walker.

We saw plenty of nesting Anhinga at the terminus of the boardwalk but what really got our attention was the "alligator hole". I counted 31 alligators that had all congregated in what is apparently the equivalent of a spa for gators. They were all enjoying the muddy, wet area - some napping, some climbing over their friends to get to a better spot, some just watching the people watching them. Unreal. As we took the return loop, we encountered two alligators who had decided they would rather sunbathe on the cement walkway than on the mud. People were walking right next to them! Uh, I'm thinking these are wild animals, not house pets. We walked waaaaay around the one that was still there by the time we got to him. Apparently they are used to humans and could care less, but still....I didn't stand around and strike up a conversation with him.

We are really excited to go back today and see more of the park. We are leaving early, taking picnic lunch and dinner, making a day of it. The park is so huge that we will only be seeing the part that is accessible from Homestead area. It will be another full day trip to go to the area west of here and we could easily make a third day also. This was so not what we expected. So far it is beautiful, informative, educational, amazing and a look into an ecosystem that was almost lost. The Florida everglades are the only everglades in the world, and what remains is only 1/5th of what was originally here before man decided to "drain the swamp". You can hardly imagine the damage that has been done to the planet, the impact on ground water and filtration of water that eventually moves out into the ocean. It is a treasure and a privilege to see and experience. Who knew?

Chapter 18

Wild Things and Wild Times

Wow! We just got to our current stop, Labelle, Florida and it looks like we're in for cooler temperatures and quieter times. We're ready for a vacation to rest up from our "vacation within a vacation".

During our stay outside the Everglades, we left the motor home and went to Islamorada to meet our friends Anne Marie and Wayne while they vacationed there at the Chesapeake Resort. What a beautiful place and what a great time! The resort had a sandy beach, turquoise blue waters, and nice rooms with garden or ocean views and included breakfast on the patio overlooking the ocean. We explored the area by kayak with a paddle through the Mangrove tunnels and out onto the bay then went to a great place to watch the sunset. After that we ate at a famous fish restaurant on the key. The next day we headed for Key West with a stop at Deer Key to see the sweet little endangered Key Deer. Wayne knew just where to look for them and they were so tame! I was concerned Wayne was going to have to return the rental car with hoof prints on it.

Ok, a great, fun day with friends at Key West…let me sum it up: it was a lot like New Orleans and as far as Joe and I were concerned, fun; saw it once that's good enough. It's a great place for party people and if Austin, Texas has the slogan "Keep Austin Weird", I think Key West beat them to it. We took the "Conch Train" tour and learned that Key West once succeeded from the Union to protest the lack of support for their most important industry, tourism. Residents attacked the Navy base with stale Cuban bread, on the premise that when Cuban bread goes stale it's pretty much like a missile. We saw the flag of the Republic and the official motto, "Where others fail, we secede." The infant country quickly surrendered and then applied for US foreign aid, as a defeated enemy of the United States. You gotta' love it.

Well, we did the tourist stuff – picture at the buoy marking the southernmost point of the continental U.S.; saw the 6–toed cats at Hemingway's house, had a drink at Sloppy Joe's Bar, watched our step as we skirted around the roosters who enjoy status as a protected species. There are chickens everywhere, crowing, scratching, holding up traffic. It is a seriously weird place.

All week it was hot, hot, hot. Sunny days gave way to humid evenings. After returning to Homestead from the Keys we got another lousy night's sleep at our RV Park. You know, when anyplace has a disclaimer that there are no refunds for any reason….you probably should be thinking that was posted for a purpose. This place had a Tiki Hut bar in the middle of the park that was open to the public. One thing about karaoke, some people can only sing when they drink and they shouldn't sing OR drink. It was noisy and rowdy every night. We were glad we were gone for 3 days of our stay. On our last full day we took a drive to the other Visitor Centers of the Everglades. By the time our week was up I'd say we had done the Everglades and the Keys pretty darn well. The weather was perfect for both. We saw SO many alligators-alligators sunbathing, laying on the walking paths, in the road, in water, swimming, lounging, and yes, roaring….in case you're tempted to forget these are wild animals, just tick one off.

On the way back from the westerly Glades, we sought out the Cuban restaurant that Anne Marie and Wayne had found on their way back to Fort Lauderdale. We had asked a store owner in Key West for a recommendation for a good Cuban restaurant and her answer was, "Well, if you like sweet, grease and fried go for Cuban food." But Anne Marie and Wayne wanted to try it anyway and they had a great meal. We thought it was good too although we weren't sure exactly what all we were eating. Our waitress was very helpful and her English was very good. I think I committed some kind of Cuban food faux pas by dumping the beans into the rice – our waitress looked a bit appalled, but it was tasty.

Last night was quite a sendoff from the RV Park – Bar was open until 2 a.m. even though there was a tremendous rain storm that lasted all night. The last party people left after 2 a.m. and the first 'early up and out' people were revving trucks about 4 a.m. Between the noise and the rainstorm we were feeling pretty bleary eyed when we hooked up and hit the road. By the way, I can't feel too bad about the rain. Yesterday one of the Rangers told us the last rain was in September 2012. Even though it was still raining off and on, the drive to Labelle was enjoyable with many, many beautiful southern Florida birds and lots of scenic views. We skirted the base of Lake Okeechobee and got to our current location about 2 p.m. We got set up, ate our leftover Cuban food and were in for the night. Nice and quiet here and I think we're going to need a good night's sleep.

American Icon – (Buoy, not us)

LaBelle Florida and Environs

Well, this park is much quieter than the rowdy place we were
before. I think we'll be happy to catch up on our sleep, bill paying
and laundry. But this morning we got up early to go to the 8 a.m.
breakfast here in the park. They do a big breakfast for $3/person with
pancakes, eggs, sausage, biscuit and gravy and a chance to meet other
people here. We were late (8:07) and the last in line. We soon
discovered that we didn't do it right. First you're supposed to pick a
spot and put your silverware down, so asked if we could join a
gentleman who was already there. He said we could go ahead and get
in line because Aces were up. I thought he might have a little
dementia but as we made our way through the line I realized that each
table had a playing card on the end and the tables were being called
by their "card". Duh.

After breakfast we decided to see what's here. In two words: not
much. We drove on to Fort Myers which is about 30 miles away.
This weekend is their big Electric Parade. Fort Myers was the winter
home of Thomas Edison and the parade in his honor is in its 75th year.
Apparently this is a BIG DEAL. We pulled into the parking structure
as most all parking spots were roped off. Due to the special event
parking was $5.00 and the attendant warned us that if we stayed after
4 p.m. we'd be blocked in until 11 p.m. after the parade and
fireworks. We wandered through the Craft Show and walked
downtown. After that we decided that staying for another four hours
just to be at the start of the parade, then standing for two hours for the
parade, then fireworks…..nope. We'll look for pictures on line.

My cousin told us that the pizza mogul, Tom Monaghan,
established a community about 25 miles from here - Ave Maria, FL.
It is a Roman Catholic University (built with the goal of rivaling
Notre Dame in Indiana) and a huge Catholic Church in the center of

town surrounded by shops and housing developments. We decided to go there for church and to see the community. The church totally dominates the landscape - you can see it for miles.

We attended the 5 p.m. Mass which was the most formal service I've ever attended. 1 hour and 20 minutes – It lasted so long I thought maybe I was in an old time protestant service! Going to church for Catholics is like old married people sex: get in, get out, everybody gets something out of it and hopefully you feel loved when it's over. Anyway, this service was complete with Gregorian chants, incense, Latin and set in a stunning church that Joe thought was right out of Star Wars and I characterized as "great Cathedrals of the middle ages meet the Industrial Age". Hard to describe but it features exposed steel beams inside and out and has won architectural awards for design. The art was amazing.

Speaking of art, afterwards we stopped across the street from the church at the pizza place. It was a little strange to be in a restaurant that featured religious art as the décor. It was fine, although Joe said it was a little difficult to use the urinal with a picture of the Virgin Mary right next to him. A very large rendering of the Last Supper decorated the hallway to the restrooms. Unusual. But the pizza was good!

Beaufort says: "OH the Humanity!!"

Well, we pulled into LaBelle, Florida last week and it has been one eventful happening after the next. Last weekend we got an overview of the area and visited the church at Ave Maria. We were hoping to hear from our friends George and Carol who were thinking of visiting us at some point on their Florida trip. They had been in LaBelle many times as they used to store their boat in the boatyard near here. Monday morning I got a call from Carol. They were coming our way; I asked what day they thought they'd be here and she said they were on their way right then! I didn't have much on hand as we had gone to the local grocery store here and nearly fainted at the prices. I really didn't buy anything to eat but the Flamingo Express was fairly presentable and I figured we'd wing it for meals.

We had a great time with George and Carol. They decided to stay at a local motel so we didn't have them bunking with us but we had lunch when they got here and made some plans for their visit. Tuesday we went to the Edison and Ford Winter Estates, Museum and Gardens for a beautiful day of history, flowers, trees, plants and wonderful outdoor weather. The temperatures were perfect, the company enjoyable and we made plans to go to the zoo at Naples, FL on Wednesday.

On Wednesday our friends discovered that their room would not be available for another night's stay because the motel was booked full for the upcoming Swamp Cabbage Festival. No, seriously. Swamp Cabbage Festival is a real thing. (More about that later). So, they decided they had to move on and Joe and I went ahead with the day at the zoo. For a small zoo, the Naples Zoo and Caribbean Gardens is a gem. They have some very rare animals, including the Honey Badger. Their tough hide allows them to raid active beehives, hence the name. The Honey Badger looks like a cross between a skunk and a badger and stinks like a mink. Interesting but better observed while standing upwind from them.

The zoo offers programs about every half hour and does a great job of education with entertainment. The Malaysian Tigers were absolutely gorgeous and we got to see them up close when they got their 4 p.m. snack. We noticed that lovely outdoor tables for a dinner party had been set up just a few feet from the tiger enclosure. We could see a number of challenges with staging an outdoor dinner there. First of all, birds fly over all the time. Secondly, it could be disconcerting to eat dinner when across the way the tigers are looking at you like you should be on their menu. We were told it was for a "private party". Ok, guess I'm happy we were not invited.

The rest of the week went by so quickly! Next thing we knew it was here! The annual LaBelle Swamp Cabbage Festival. Not a lot was happening on Friday but you could tell there was excitement in the air! What, you say, is a swamp cabbage? That was our first question too. Turns out that what you might pay big bucks for in a gourmet section as "hearts of palm", is locally called swamp cabbage and celebrated every year the last weekend in February. An actual palm tree is cut down and the inner part or "heart" is what is used in various recipes. No one could really tell us how it tastes, so we were determined to find out for ourselves.

Well, we didn't get out early enough on Saturday to avoid the bridge closure, so we ended up taking a tour of the countryside to circumvent the bridge and get into town. Luckily, the parade had just started and we found a "sort of" parking spot on the grass at the end of a public lot and didn't miss anything.

You might think a Swamp Cabbage parade would be hokey but no! It was quite the doings with tractors pulling decorated floats, marchers, bands, swamp buggies, horses, the King and Queen and of course, lots of palm branches decorating everything.

LaBelle was so chock full of people, cars, motorcycles and horses that we just left our car where it was and walked towards the area set up for the main events. We took in the car show (Joe's favorite) on the way and then scoped out the various stands selling swamp cabbage delicacies. We decided to go for the swamp cabbage chowder and the fritters. Unfortunately, after standing in line for about half an hour we were told that the electricity had gone out and they weren't selling chowder. However they were using the deep fat fryers so??? Anyway, no chowder but we took our cardboard container of 'hot out of the fryer' fritters served with a side of "secret sauce" and wedged ourselves in at a very crowded table in the pavilion nearby. To tell the truth, I'm not positive there was any swamp cabbage in the fritters. They basically tasted like hush puppies. There might have been a faint cabbage flavor and there might have been some tiny bits of palm but I can't really swear to it.

Well, luckily there was much more to capture our attention. We heard the bugle call alerting us to place our bets and choose our armadillo. The little guys were hoisted out of their happy little straw filled beds and lined up to start. Unfortunately, armadillos are not the most enthusiastic racers on earth. As a matter of fact it was really hard to tell who was winning. I jumped up and down and shouted when they announced number 6 was the winner! Our armadillo won, or so we thought. Turned out number 4 was the actual winner; number 6 refused to trot across the racecourse. You can't win 'em all. We were somewhat ashamed of ourselves that we had exploited poor, wild caught armadillos even though it was for a good cause: fundraiser for the local Rotary Club. When our own little resident armadillo heard about what had gone on he was furious. He hasn't said a word to us all night, that's how we know he's really mad. At least, we think so. Come to think of it he hasn't said anything for the entire trip….But Beaufort has every reason to be upset. Joe was talking to one of the armadillo handlers and asked him how he was qualified to race them. Turns out, if you can catch one – you're qualified. This fellow had caught several at night when armadillos are most active. Apparently their eye sight isn't really great. He snuck up on one and when the poor thing finally realized someone was there he jumped straight up in the air four feet. That might have been our losing armadillo - suffering from post-traumatic stress disorder. The good news is, after the festival all the little guys will be returned to the wild, having had all the crickets they can eat.

We rounded out the festival with a tour of the booths set up by various organizations and vendors. Joe sampled the local Catholic Church's famous strawberry shortcake but I was bummed out because they served it on those nasty little round sponge cakes from the grocery store. Ick. We also were entertained by a really good band and then the Cloggers. Clogging is like tap dancing on steroids. I don't know how those kids did it in this heat.

The heat finally did us in and we walked back to our car by way of the motorcycle show which wasn't so much a show as a bunch of cycles all parked on one street. We were only there for four hours but between the heat and the excitement, we were toast. Only one disappointment – we went back to get our tee shirts with the slogan "eat a tree" and they were sold out. Joe did get his official armadillo race tee shirt though. He just can't wear it in front of Beaufort.

A Bad Day Retired Beats a Good Day Working

(A day in which the GPS lies, traffic snarls and Lana has several bouts of "stupid"…)

Yes, that was my day yesterday. We had enjoyed a really nice week of camping with my cousin John R. and his wife Sally at Lake Manatee State Park, Bradenton. Funny thing about Lake Manatee – no manatees. There is a dam that prevents them from reaching the lake. But it is a nice park with several walking trails and a lovely quiet campground.

We got to celebrate John R's step-father, our dear "Uncle" Roy's 90th birthday while we were there and also visit with my 92 year old cousin, Louise, who lives in Bradenton. We did a bunch of Florida things - went to the beach, the flea market and out for lunch, out for dinner, had a picnic and a barbeque. The week went by so fast! We went our separate ways from the State Park on Friday morning. Joe and I headed to Tampa to an RV Park that had been recommended to us by some campers we met in LaBelle. It is one of the biggest places I've ever seen: a combo campground, RV sales and service, consignment center and I guess you'd say it's a conference center. Really unusual; they throw in your breakfast and lunch if you camp here and you get a newspaper delivered every day. So we got settled in on Friday, made a quick shopping run, got some dinner and called it a day.

Saturday morning we talked about our plans for Tampa. We knew we wanted to go to Busch Gardens Park but on Saturday we wanted to either go north to Weeki Watchee Springs or out to the coast and beaches. It was one of those 'heads or tails' toss sort of things and we decided to go to the beach. That was our first mistake. Let me tell you, Tampa traffic is just awful. Four lanes in both directions and everyone here drives like a homicidal maniac. We got stuck in traffic just trying to get to the beach and probably at that point we could have changed plans but we soldiered on. A twelve mile drive took about an hour and a half. We then discovered that the bridge over to the islands on the other side of Tampa Bay was a dreaded, yes dare I say it, TOLL bridge. You may recall that my husband will not pay a toll. Soooo-we drove all the way back north in bumper to bumper traffic inching our way from one traffic light to the next back up to the next bridge which was FREE.

When we finally got to the shore we discovered two things: 1.) You couldn't see the ocean and 2.) If you got to a beach where you COULD see the ocean you had to pay for very expensive parking. It took all afternoon to get through traffic and back to the Clearwater area where I had scoped out a church that had a 5:30 p.m. service. Good thing we started heading that way when we did because again, it took like an hour and a half to cover twenty miles. I had set the GPS and once we got off the islands it took us on a merry chase of turns, jogs, merges and finally an announcement, "You have reached your destination." Except we weren't at a church, we were in the parking lot of a medical facility. We pulled around the corner and still couldn't see a church anywhere. Joe backed up in traffic and was behaving in a very un-Christian manner regarding not finding the church. And he implied strongly that it was MY fault. Well, luckily my new Stupid Phone has internet, so I tried looking up the church to see if I could figure out the correct address.

Yay!! Found the church's website. Except as I looked at the website it appeared the service had been at 4:00 p.m. not 5:30. Oops. It was already after 5. We sat in the parking lot a few minutes trying to find another church with a later service then finally gave up and pulled back out into the heavy traffic. At that point we realized there was so much traffic because the CHURCH parking lot across the street had just started emptying out. That would be the church we had been looking for, as it turns out. I don't know how we didn't see it.

We had both had enough traffic, frustration and crankiness for one day. We had one last mission left for the day: Pie. Years ago we had found a wonderful pie place in Clearwater and by searching the internet I was pretty sure I had located it in their new location. More stop and go traffic but finally, the highlight of our day!!! We found the pie place. They still sold pies by the piece or a whole pie to go. The way the day had gone we decided to go for the whole pie. We then got stuck on a bridge for so long that I came close to eating it before we got across town. It was totally **insane** the amount of traffic on a Saturday night! I can't imagine weekly rush hour. Fist fights must break out if not actual shootings. We got back to the RV tired and hungry. Never got to the beach, missed church, pie was getting warm and some kind of tiny little bugs had invaded the motor coach while we were gone. I smacked bugs, warmed up some leftovers and again-highlight of the day: pie. Thank goodness for pie.

Joe was so tired that he went to bed early and I was trying to be very quiet not to wake him up. Naturally I made as much noise as a freight train being driven by a rhinoceros since I was *trying* to be quiet. For my final screw up of the day, I set down my glass of water on the table-the same table where the computer and my phone were sitting-and promptly knocked the glass over. I lunged onto the bench seat desperately trying to save the computer and mop up the mess. This of course, resulted in also getting the seat soaking wet. As I backed off the bench I somehow caught my toe in the edge, very effectively separating the toenail from the toe. Ow.

This was one of those days that I had to really remind myself that a bad day retired beats a good day working anytime....

Sometimes when you move and do a lot of things in a short period of time it gets a little disorienting. Just three days ago we were still in Tampa at Lazy Days Campground. We spent our 2nd day at Busch Gardens with absolutely beautiful weather and saw everything we missed the first day as well as did a few things a second time. The ice show there and the live animal acts are really incredible. Both were the best I've ever seen. Nothing is the same as Disney, but Busch Gardens is really a nice place to visit.

We left Tampa in the morning and by afternoon we were at Stephen Foster Cultural Center State Park, White Springs, FL. First a word about White Springs: it is basically a ghost town that hasn't quite given up the ghost. It was the very first "tourist" destination in Florida; Sulphur springs that had been known to Native Americans for the healing powers of the water. Today's springs look a lot more like a cesspool. The old spring house built in the 1900's to replace an original log cabin bath house of the 1800's has been preserved as a historical site but peering down into the waters we saw floating trash, aerosol cans, beer cans, plastic bags as well as natural debris. Hard to believe people once swarmed here to bathe in the waters much less DRINK the water. About 1970 was the end of the era that once boasted something like fourteen luxury hotels. One hotel is still standing. The brick walls are crumbling but the sign out front is still presentable. On the door is a hand lettered sign that says, "Closed for renovation; open in a couple weeks." I don't think so…

So, White Springs has tried to reinvent itself with what it has-the Suwannee River. The State Park there along the riverside is really unusual. It has a Carillion tower that plays Stephen Foster melodies four times a day, and chimes the quarter, half and hours during the daylight hours. The connection is that Foster's most famous song was about the Suwannee River, although it turns out that Foster never saw the river and just picked the name to fit the music. That hasn't stopped the state of Florida from capitalizing on the famous song and the songwriter. There is an absolutely gorgeous museum commemorating Stephen Foster and his music, all housed in a splendid recreated plantation home; there are acres of trails, river walks, a craft shop and several small buildings that house individual craftsmen who smith, spin, weave, create jewelry and also play music for your entertainment. It's unlike any campgrounds we've been to, that's for sure.

We pulled in at Stephen Foster SP to be serenaded by the 4 p.m. Carillion bells concert then ventured into town just in time to get to the Visitor's Center next to the springs before it closed for the day. It too is a really nice, very new building with displays and lots of information. You just have to wonder who decided to put such a fantastic facility in a one horse town. White Springs has some of the poorest looking folks we've seen in all our travels. There are a few nice newer homes and a couple of well-kept Victorian houses but for the most part the phrase that comes to mind is "crushing poverty". Most of "downtown" looks like a Wild West ghost town until you get a couple of blocks off the main four corners and find yourself at "Fat Belly's".

Well, we have the requisite "fat bellies" so we decided we'd better try Fat Belly's restaurant the next day. Mmmmmmmm. Breakfast was only $3.99 for meat, eggs, and your choice of potatoes or grits. Plus toast! It was so good we went back for the barbeque for dinner. We each got a plate piled high with meat plus garlic bread, fries, and baked beans – and it included sweet tea for only $7.99. I don't know how they stay in business.

I felt somewhat justified in eating all that barbeque as we had hiked for miles along the Florida Trail all day. I must have waddled off a few calories because we followed trails along the river, then down steep banks, up hills, through sand and forest and muddy back tracks. It was a beautiful day to be outdoors and periodically we could hear the distant bells of the Carillion. Memorable.

The next morning we started back towards Michigan and spent the day on the road. We found a good stopping point at Cartersville, GA which was none too soon after getting through Atlanta traffic. Our friend Theresa tried to tell us to go around the Atlanta area on an alternate route but no..... I'll just say Joe and I are still speaking to each other and we DID miss rush hour so it wasn't a total disaster. (Avoid Atlanta). Just before getting to the campground there was a good fueling stop to get in and out so we stopped to get gas. I was tending the gas pump when a lady approached me. She seemed very nervous and she was holding her driver's license and social security card. She was very apologetic and said repeatedly she didn't want to "bother me none" but her story was that she had been in an accident, totaled her car, gone to the hospital and was now in her friend's car but needed 'just a couple of gallons of gas' to make it home. She showed me her ID and promised she'd send me the money as she 'had a paycheck waitin' on me at home'. I didn't have any cash but when Joe came back to the gas pump I asked him to give her some money. He gave her a $10 bill and when she wanted our address to pay it back to us, he declined. Guess we both thought that was 10 bucks we'd never see again anyway. She put a couple gallons of gas in the vehicle and drove off.

I was so mad at myself that I am such a sucker... by the time we got to the KOA campground I was kicking myself that I'm still so gullible at my age. But yet, the lady seemed so sincere and it looked like a hospital ID band on her wrist....I just wished there were some way I could know if I had just been really stupid. I had made our camping reservation on line and couldn't get my KOA 10% discount to work. Big deal - $3.80 but I asked the owner why I never got an ID card and couldn't get my discount. She very kindly looked up my membership and then told me there was a 26% special on camping and since I'd reserved on line, she'd apply the discount to my account. The total came to $12.00, which she credited back to my

VISA. I must have looked like a complete idiot as I got tears in my eyes but I stood there feeling as if I'd just had my answer as to whether or not I'd been stupid or done the right thing.....

Chapter 19

The Flamingo Express at Rest

I thought perhaps I should make it clear that our hapless adventures with (and without) the motorhome do not end once we pull into our driveway. Oh, no. We are quite capable of major screw-ups on the road **and** at home.

We were so fortunate to get back during a short weather window before there was a state by state horror show of winds, freezing rain and snow. We opened the season for a KOA in Indiana on the way home and considering the nasty weather they've had since, I suspect we've been their only customer so far this year. We got home fairly early in the afternoon which is ideal because it gives us a chance to solve any problems we find on homecoming before we are completely dead dog tired and while it is still daylight.

Joe had done a great job of wrapping up the house before we had left so no leaks, no disasters. Not like last year when we came home to discover we needed $3000.00 in roof repairs. Ahhh, but not so fast! Yes, we did leave the water turned off which was good! But Joe also disconnected the hoses to the washer, which would have been good if he had remembered to reconnect them before turning the water back on. So, before we could unload the motorhome we had to move the washer and dryer and mop up a few gallons of water. The good news: it was CLEAN water (could have been worse) and I've been trying to get Joe to help me pull out the washer/dryer to thoroughly clean behind them for longer than I want you to know. So, we started our time back at home with a really, really clean laundry room.

Joe had been griping about how uncomfortable the motor home furniture was. I really thought it was ok and we were usually out a good part of every day, so it was no big deal. We no more than got settled in than Joe got really antsy to check out replacement furniture. I have a rule – if I don't do the work, I don't criticize. So, we started looking at dining furniture and a new sofa and side chair. This, of course led to having to replace the carpeting. Turns out, that was a really good idea. When Joe took the dinette booth off from the living area tip out room, guess what? Well, I'll tell you – I wasn't the one to point it out. For forty-five years I'm always the one who says, "I think that bowed ceiling is going to come down." Or…"I think that loose area on the family room wall is something that we need to check." And…"Don't you think we should get the septic tank pumped before the graduation party?" These queries are always met with a standard response, "Nah." So, after years of collapsed ceilings, termite infested walls and sewage flooded back yards, I am reluctant to point out things that I think might be problematic. Luckily, this time Joe was the one to say, "Uh, oh. That doesn't look good."

Over the winter I thought that our living room slide was tipping farther and farther when we put it out and had developed a certain "clunk". Turned out there was a good reason. The plates that hold the inner wall of the slide to the motor coach had completely fractured. Hence the "clunk". At some point we would have been sitting in the slide room and found ourselves on the ground. Or we could have put out the slide and it would have just have kept on going

So, I guess it was good luck that Joe decided to change the furniture. The coach is already repaired and we are soon making our 3rd trip to Indiana to try to decide on furniture. It hasn't been that easy. You'd think things would be standard in a motor home but oh, no … they definitely are not. And our coach has a "raised" slide which makes installing replacement furniture even trickier. One thing we didn't think about was if we just popped in a standard sized couch we'd be left with our feet dangling about 6" off the floor when sitting.

We're finally at the point of getting carpet. Ruled out laminate (hard choice), picked out one carpeting and then changed our minds, but I think we've got it now. We found a terrific buy on a table and chairs to replace the booth dinette (which Joe hated) and once we had that it was easier to decide on colors for the chair and sofa. Now, the only trick is for Joe to get this all done before we want to leave. IF we can leave on time as it is….

It turns out that I am apparently the only person who has ever had trouble signing up for Medicare. What a hassle. You aren't supposed to sign up before 64 years and 9 months of age. OK. I went on line two days after that date, thinking this would be easy. Instead I ended up with a batch of questions. I called the local office. Unfortunately I called at four minutes before noon on a Wednesday. They close at noon on Wednesday and by the time I went through all the "press 1's" it was after noon and they were closed. OK. Tried again on Thursday. An automated voice politely informed me that my call would be answered in the order it had been received and my expected wait time would be...10...minutes...or more. No. So on Friday I called again and was flipped to the national phone line. After a very long and fruitless discussion with the phone person I requested an "in person" appointment at the Social Security office. The first appointment available is May 7. We had planned to leave on May 6. Could I go to a different office? Grand Rapids? Nope, you have to go to the office in the "region" where you are located by zip code. And guess what? I understand I can't apply for supplemental coverage until I have Medicare Part A and B, which I can't apply for until I get an appointment with Social Security. It gets better. You don't just walk in and receive a confirmation that you are signed up for A and B, you get a packet in the mail. So, I guess I'm supposed to just sit in my house waiting for that to show up. Not a workable plan for a six week road trip with no place to pick up my mail while I'm gone…just a minor little detail to straighten out.

We had made one other decision for the motor home based on happenings here at home. My Dr. had suggested that we raise the head of the bed to help with gastric reflux. We have been trying to figure out a way to do that in the motor home like we had set up our bed at home. After our experience with our bed at home we've decided to forget it in the motor home.

About a week ago I had a really tough time getting to sleep and tossed and turned until well after midnight. I had finally fallen asleep and about five minutes later I was rocketed out of bed at the sound of a tremendous crash. I had thrown off the covers and was on my feet screaming, "What was that?" before Joe got his head off the pillow. We checked outside to see if a tree limb had hit the house, the basement to see if the furnace exploded, the garage, upstairs – everywhere. We thought about a plane breaking the sound barrier (unlikely). My heart was pounding and I couldn't think straight. I told Joe that the explosion sounded like it was right under our bed. He finally looked under the bed and discovered that the leg under the head of the bed had slipped off the board he had propped it up on and it had dropped about four inches to the floor. I assume our house is basically standing still. Since the motor coach moves, there is no way I'm going to have the bed in there propped up. I'm amazed one of us didn't have a heart attack.

So, we've got a few weeks to get everything straightened out here and then back on the road for our first extended "springtime" trip. We've had a few setbacks, a few lucky breaks and there are three baskets of clean laundry tripping us in the bedroom while awaiting return to the motorhome. We'll see what happens between now and the day we pull out for another adventure on the road.

See you next time!

June 17, 1967 and June 17, 2017

Photo credit: Anne Marie Hovey

A Few Notes

As our first few trips were some years ago now, the RV Parks may have changed name, ownership or amenities. It happens. Also, some attractions may no longer be as stated. So, if you have your heart set on any of the places I have mentioned, check it out first.

I use a commercially available routing and planning tool to map out our trips by putting in the starting and ending points and adding the sights we want to include. We plan RV travel with a formula many use: 300 miles a day and stop no later than 3 p.m. We have certainly gone around our own rule, especially making a quick trip back home. But for the purpose of leisurely travel allow plenty of time if possible. Usually we will plan three days, two nights as a minimum stop for any destination. Getting set up in the afternoon usually gives us time to enjoy the park or scope out part of the city or attraction. We then have a full day for the area and on the third day most campgrounds require a checkout between 11 a.m. and 1 p.m. so that takes up most of Day 3 getting ready to hit the road again.

For each trip I have a three ring binder with pages for each stop: Reservation and contact information (including if it has been paid or partially paid), area information/tours, tickets etc. and a printed map in case the GPS fails. Joe puts the next destination in the GPS the night before we depart to check the mileage, time of arrival and confirm we are going to the correct place. (Yes, I have in fact goofed that up before.) You might prefer a spread sheet, a file on your computer or a road map and a pencil. It's your trip, do what works for you.

Recommendation: Read the ratings, look at the website pictures and get a visual overview of a campground you are considering. We've stayed at some rated 10/10/10, best in all categories that I would never recommend to anyone. And conversely, been surprised at the amazing places that weren't so highly rated.

Different things appeal to different travelers. Traveling with children means you'll want fun "kid activities", playground, pool, beach, attractions. Older travelers may value a quiet park with fewer activities while others are willing to pay more for lots of things to do and social opportunities. WIFI, shopping, laundry facilities - all of these can be important. City, County, State and National Parks offer unique experiences and the budget minded will want to check out National Wildlife Refuges, National Forest lands, the Bureau of Land Management as well as local and State campgrounds. Keep in mind that size of your rig is often limiting factor especially with National, Parks.

As of this writing there are still some Walmart locations that allow you to camp in the parking lot as well as some Cracker Barrel Restaurants. Casinos sometimes offer camping in the parking lot or even a have well-priced RV park at their location. . I can't say it enough: it's your trip so do what you enjoy. We've seen folks in high end million dollar rigs having a miserable time at a five star resort and we've seen van campers having the time of their lives "roughing it". Whatever you decide -

Be well, stay safe and Happy Travels!

Printed in Great Britain
by Amazon

61982786R00108